The Road
That Has No End

Tim Travis

"How we traded in our ordinary lives for a global
bicycle touring adventure"

Down The Road Publishing
Indianapolis, Indiana

The Road That Has No End
How we traded in our ordinary lives for a global bicycle
touring adventure.
By Tim Travis

Published by:
Down The Road Publications
2346 S. Lynhurst Dr. Suite C-101
Indianapolis, IN 46241
www.downtheroad.org/publishing

ISBN 0-9754427-0-8

Library of Congress Control Number: 2004112503

Photo Credit: All photography by Tim and Cindie Travis unless
noted

Visit the Travis' ongoing travels at:
www.downtheroad.org

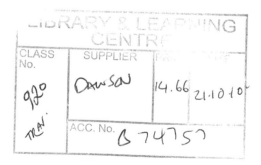

Dedication

To all the wonderful people of the world who I have met and learned from while traveling. I will forever appreciate our differences and take comfort in our similarities.

Cindie would like to dedicate this book to her Aunt Fran and Uncle Vic who introduced her to camping at an early age and to her twin sister Cherie who inspired her to keep a daily journal.

Table of Contents

1 Leaving It All Behind

Travelers call the road home, and our home is a road that has no end. Travelers wake to an itch, a need to trade the weight of material possessions, creature comforts and security for what is unknown, often uncomfortable and sometimes dangerous. In exchange, they experience new cultures, see beautiful places the world has to offer, and learn about themselves in the process. The trade is well worth it. As you read this, I'm probably on the road.

I began my obsession with traveling in grade school. My father returned from a business trip in Germany with a wall map of Europe. I found it alluring that the map was entirely in the German language. My imagination was sparked! Maps, globes and world atlases mesmerized me.

I scoured my middle school library looking for books about distant countries and cultures. I can remember playing a game at the library. I would spin the globe and shut my eyes. Then, I would stop it with my finger and see what country I had randomly selected. Next, I would look the country up in the encyclopedia and search for all of the books that I could find about it.

Soon the answers I was looking for were not to be found in Indiana. The cornfields of Indiana can be a long way from anything. Little did I know that some day I would be riding my bicycle through remote villages in Guatemala or discussing politics with impoverished farmers in Nicaragua. Patience is essential for a traveling man.

Background

Born in 1966, I grew up in Greenwood, Indiana in a good home with two loving parents. I found my calling at the age of eleven when I became a cyclist. My parents were wise to nurture this instinct in me. I firmly believe that my involvement in cycling kept me out of serious trouble.

I started riding bicycles in the mid-1970's with a Campy five-speed bike, wool shorts and one of those funny leather helmets that cyclists wore back then. The bicycle racing movie *"Breaking Away,"* hit the theaters and I quickly fell into racing. I was immersed in racing until I graduated from Indiana University in 1991 with a bachelor's degree in Physical Education. Competing on a bicycle taught me many things, including riding techniques and mechanical skills I now use in my daily life on the road. More importantly, racing taught me how far I could push myself physically. This foundation prepared me for a future full of biking in foul weather and endless mountain climbs.

Once I was finished with undergraduate school, I was free to roam. I left Indiana permanently and headed west. I traveled by bicycle and worked in several different states in the western US. I existed on the least amount of money possible. I drifted around looking for work in each town, saved up a little money and moved on. This may sound romantic; but in reality, it was difficult. This kind of living can exhaust even a young man. I learned the ropes of basic survival and hard living. Looking ragged and being treated as an outcast taught me much about society. Many people looked down on me because I looked poor. They did not judge me on my actions but the way I looked. A few people didn't notice my appearance and saw me as an equal. This served as a strong reminder of a value I had always known: avoid bias based on appearances.

I settled in Arizona where the climate and mountains suited me. I lived in Prescott for ten years except for two years of graduate school at Northern Arizona University (NAU) in Flagstaff. It was at NAU that I met Cindie's twin sister, Cherie, and husband, Scott. They introduced me to Cindie who was living in New Mexico at the time.

Cindie was energetic and loved the outdoors. She was born in 1961 and grew up on the east coast. Cindie had previously attended NAU and finished with a Bachelor of Science in Geology in 1984. She was working as a geologist in Albuquerque when I met her.

Cindie and I had a two-wheeled romance. When I met Cindie, she owned a mountain bike. Our first date was a mountain bike ride in Flagstaff. During this date, she crashed and bruised her knee badly. I helped her up and put her back on her bike. I wondered if she would finish out our ride or go home crying. She thought about quitting for a moment but, instead, finished the ride. Years later, Cindie told me this was a tender moment for her and explained that when I comforted her I encouraged her to do what she had previously thought impossible. This was a defining moment in our relationship for both of us.

Early in our relationship, I took Cindie on her first bike tour around the Yucatan Peninsula in southern Mexico. I took the cheap way down, riding a bus to Cancun, and met Cindie in the airport well after dark. I unpacked her bike and assembled it. She asked if we were going to one of the famous beaches. She was excited to have a romantic get-away. I have never liked touristy beach resorts and told her that we were going in the opposite direction. Cancun is only an airport to me. She asked where we were staying for the night. I answered, "I will figure that out when we get there." She nervously followed me into the Mexican darkness. She must have trusted me a lot to have done this. We found a construction site and set the tent up. In the morning, we met friendly Mexican workers and over a long conversation shared our coffee. She saw that traveling could be more than glitzy beach resorts.

A few months later, she bought a used road bike. She learned to draft and ride pace lines on the roads of New Mexico. I saw a lot of potential in her as a cyclist.

After the trip to Mexico, I bought the first motor vehicle I had owned in five years; a 24-foot 1976 Ford Recreational

Vehicle (RV) that leaked five different colors of fluids and burned $10 in gasoline for every hour driven. It was old when I bought it and literally falling apart when I sold it years later. I had two repair manuals and learned how to keep it working more or less. The RV would play an unexpected but important role in making my dream come true in the future.

When I finished graduate school, I moved out of my apartment in Flagstaff and permanently into my RV. I was detached from the earth, living mobile and rent-free. I could have gone anywhere I liked, but I returned to Prescott, Arizona. To this day, I think of it as a nearly perfect place for a cyclist to live. It has great weather, endless mountain bike trails and challenging road rides. My RV was fully self-contained including a hot shower and refrigerator. I set it up so I could park free and ride my bicycle for transportation, including to and from work.

Cindie was able to find a good job in a geologic consulting firm in Prescott, and moved into the RV with me. This lasted several months but eventually we rented a house. Back then, we owned many possessions and had trouble fitting into this small space. We continued using the RV for weekend getaways. In the winter, we would go to Phoenix and participate in group bicycle rides. In the summer, we would go to Flagstaff and mountain bike in the cool mountain temperatures.

Everything changed when Cindie wanted to buy a tandem (bicycle built for two) with me. I knew, as a life long cyclist, that this was the ultimate sign of commitment. Wedding rings are liquid. They can be bought and sold easily. Tandem bicycles are individual machines that fit two specific people in terms of two sizes, style and color. I am 6'4" (1.93 meters) and Cindie is 5'7" (1.70 meters). Tandem bikes can also be quite expensive. For these reasons, it takes months of planning to buy one. A tandem is nearly impossible to sell. Where would you find two people of the same height and bicycle preferences? Buying a tandem bicycle means two people plan on riding together for life. The idea of marriage comes to each of us in its own unique way, strangely enough; this was how it started to form, for me. I knew that it was time to ask her to marry me.

I proposed during a bike ride. I simply pulled up next to her and asked. "Will you marry me?" We were married in a Las Vegas drive thru called "The Tunnel of Love." We rode up on single bikes, the Justice of the peace spoke, and we switched to our tandem and rode away. We have been

Our Bicycle Wedding in a Las Vegas Drive Thru.

joined in this symbolic way ever since. We don't have to be on the same bike to be connected.

We spent our honeymoon in the Seattle, Washington area touring on our tandem. We enjoyed three weeks of good weather while camping and riding our loaded bike. The seeds of an epic journey were planted while we casually drifted past the incredible scenery. Neither of us wanted it to end. We talked unceasingly about what it would be like to keep going.

First, we had to go back to Prescott and resume our "normal" lives. We bought a house and settled into our jobs and daily routines. Cindie continued her work as a geologist, and I worked as a Special Education Teacher in a local school. After a short time, the road would be whispering in my ear again.

Five Years Before We Left

Occasionally I would say to Cindie, "What if we left and bike toured until retirement." At this point, we didn't have the necessary funds, so the whole concept seemed unrealistic. Time would work this dream into a reality, but it took baby steps.

We were already saving money. Our original goal was to save enough to pay cash for a new truck. This was logical because Cindie used her four-wheel-drive truck for work. She was always going to remote locations on sketchy roads. Our thinking was that it was only a matter of time before age rendered her truck undependable. When the time came to replace it, we didn't want to go into debt.

Saving money made sense to both of us, but I was thinking of something better than a truck. I always had the dream of seeing the world and that requires money. We worked out how much we were earning and our expenses. The difference was surprising. We were amazed at how cheaply we could live. Cindie calculated a monthly budget to pay our mortgage and other essential expenses. She then added enough money so that we could be comfortable and have small extras. She calculated that if we could tighten the belt a little more we could live on 25% of our income. The remaining 75% could be saved every month. We stuck to this budget for five years. In fact, whenever we received pay raises we didn't increase our living budget, but instead increased the percentage of our saving.

Our secret to being able to save this aggressively was simple. We cut out the big-ticket items that other couples with similar incomes were buying on credit. We never made car or credit card payments. The only debt that we allowed was the mortgage for the house. We had purchased a 1,000-square foot, two-bedroom house that was half of what we could afford. We were approved for a mortgage that would have put us into financial bondage. We had no use for a showy house with 3,000-square feet of living area. The payments would have been a substantial percentage of our income. That wasn't our American dream.

After about thirty months, we reached our original savings goal of $30,000. Now we needed to decide what to do with the money. We could buy a flashy four-wheel-drive that would be the envy of the neighborhood. We could buy many tempting toys that are essential in American culture to announce success. I kept thinking that this money could be used for something more. I told Cindie that we could use this money to travel for two or three years. She didn't believe me. Cindie had traveled to numerous countries before I met her. Her previous traveling experiences to Europe, Asia and New Zealand had always been more expensive. We compromised. We had her old truck painted and tuned up instead of buying a new one. Keeping our growing savings in the bank kept our options open. This was my first sign that Cindie was considering my dream to travel.

I started telling all of our friends that Cindie and I were going on a multi-year, around-the-world-bike tour. I even speculated the month and year that we were leaving. They would turn to Cindie and ask her for confirmation. Cindie said, "This is Tim's dream. It's good for Tim to dream, but we have a house and careers here."

I felt on my own. This didn't stop me from talking about my dream all the time. I'm sure that I annoyed many people. I couldn't help it. The idea burned inside of me. I thought that the more I talked about it the more likely it would actually happen. I thought of it as a self-fulfilling prophecy.

Leaving it all behind doesn't sound so romantic when you are the one risking everything. Cindie liked the idea of saving money and traveling. The thought of living in a tent and completely changing our lifestyle was difficult for her to accept at first.

I worked the idea into her head slowly but steadily. There were a few facts on my side. Cindie has a passion for travel. She previously had traveled by bus through numerous countries. She wanted more. She, like many Americans, was also tired of working long hours at her job. My big dream tempted her because it offered more to life. My idea promised freedom itself.

I bought every book I could find about people who had previously ridden around the world on bicycles. I made sure that these books were visible in our house. Cindie, who is an avid reader, eventually read a few of them. By reading these books, she learned that such trips are possible. I needed a tool to push her into commitment. I was getting close.

For most people, including Cindie, thinking and planning several years in advance is difficult. I needed a tangible way of showing her that we were making progress in reaching a start date. I made a calendar on our computer. It had thirty-two pages representing the number of months until the date we left. Every page had a large number at the top. The first page started with "32" and counted down every month until it reached "1." This represented the last month before we left. Instead of a random picture for decoration, I had a map of a different country every month. Under each map, I put information about the weather and the best time to visit each country. For example, the month of December had a map of Guatemala and said something like, "The dry season is from November – May. Weather-wise this is the most pleasant time to travel in Guatemala." These countries didn't flow in order, but instead randomly jumped around the globe to build excitement. At first, Cindie didn't think much of my calendar. Thirty-two pages felt thick and the number of months still looked like a lot of time to wait. I hung it up in our house and it became our working calendar. We wrote various appointments and activities on the corresponding dates and consulted it often. As time went by the numbers decreased and the stack of paper became thinner. Tearing a page off every month took on special meaning. I think that this tactile and visual reminder of time passing was powerful.

Two Years Before We Left

During the last two years, I started an extensive study of the world. I bought dozens of travel guidebooks. I always had several with me wherever I went. Friends and coworkers would become suspicious when they saw books and maps for China, Africa and Europe with me at the same time. I first read the important preliminary facts about weather, visa requirements and cost. After I gained a general idea of each region, I looked up specific places and tried to imagine what it would be like for us to be arriving on loaded bicycles. Where would we sleep, eat and use a bankcard?

Soon my desk was completely covered with maps and books. I felt as if I was back in middle school looking at the world atlas and dreaming of a world that was so far away.

This time it was much more fun; now, it could actually happen.

The internet held the most useful information. I found dozens of Web sites made by others who were riding in every country of the world. Reading their stories about cycling adventures taught me what to expect. I learned to adjust my expectations of life on the road.

The most elusive piece of the puzzle was trying to determine how much it was going to cost. I wanted to estimate how far our money would take us. This was frustrating because bicycle touring Web sites and books do not disclose detailed information about cost. The budgets suggested in the guidebooks are high. Guidebooks are designed for short-term tourists traveling by bus. The budgets in the guidebooks factor in the cost of lodging and bus tickets. We planned on camping often and riding our bikes. I felt that we could go much cheaper, but Cindie wasn't as sure. This was truly the great unknown and therefore was a source of fear. After much research and debate, Cindie and I finally settled on an annual budget of $15,000 or about $41 a day for the two of us. Next, we divided our expected savings by this estimated budget and came up with seven years.

The cost of equipment was much higher than expected which prevented us from making our savings goal. We bought high quality equipment. Our bicycles cost over US$4,000 combined; the laptop computer and digital camera cost over US$4,000 combined; panniers for both bikes cost over US$1000; tent, water filter and camp stove cost over US$1000 combined; and bike and travel clothing cost over US$1000 combined.

In total we spent over US$11,000 on equipment the first year; we originally budgeted US$6,000 for equipment. If our travel budget was off by as much, our plans could have derailed! Luckily, the daily cost of traveling turned out to be less than our original annual estimate of US$15,000.

We went over our equipment budget by US$5,000, but we ended up under our travel budget by US$5,000; therefore, we remained close to our budget for the first year.

Once we had settled on seven years, I started piecing our trip together. Nothing in my life had felt more exciting than looking at a world map and working out how much of it my wife and I would see in seven years.

Our route was based on cost effectiveness, avoiding burn out and weather patterns. The cost effectiveness boiled down to limiting flights and seeking cheaper countries.

I knew from my research that travelers' burn out is a real problem for those on multi-year trips. To avoid this I scheduled extra amounts of time for each area so we would never feel rushed. I also had the idea that we would mix difficult underdeveloped countries with developed comfortable countries. These strategies would keep our living standards changing enough to renew our interest and keep us fresh.

Paying attention to weather patterns is important in bicycle touring and is the most difficult part of the planning process. This is where my calendar with the weather came in handy. I came up with a plan that would follow the best weather around the globe.

<u>One Year Before We Left</u>

Our homemade calendar had shrunk to a dozen pieces of paper. We were down to the final year. The big "12" highlighted on the top couldn't be avoided. This short amount of time pushed the issue of commitment. If we were actually going to go through with our plan, several critical tasks had to be completed. Accomplishing these tasks would require commitment from Cindie and push us past the point of no return. We had to sell or box for storage everything we owned except what we could carry on two bicycles. In addition, we had to move out and rent our house, switch bank accounts

11

and cancel auto insurance policies. My discrete persuasion and patience was put to the test.

Previously, Cindie's first reason for not going was the lack of funds. Now, the numbers in our bank account looked good and she knew that we could reach our savings goal of $105,000 within twelve more months. This caused the true fears inside of her to surface. Completely letting go of the security and comfort of her current lifestyle was staring her in the face. Everything she was used to would be left behind. I am not exactly sure when she decided to commit fully. It was gradual. Nevertheless, I was happy when she told me she was ready to quit her job and go. She later confessed that she wanted to go on the trip while she was still willing to camp and sleep on the ground.

Once she was committed, she never looked back. She isn't a quitter. Now that we have been on the road for several years, it would be impossible to talk her out of it. She is also married to the road. A true rambling woman.

I formulated the escape plan. I truly thought of it as an escape plan because it seemed as if everyone and everything was trying to prevent us from living out our dream. Our friends outside of work told us that we were crazy and tried to convince us to keep our careers. I knew that they were only looking out for our best interests. They still didn't think we were serious. We were alone.

Going from living in a house with a car to living in a tent with a bicycle is an incredibly difficult thing to do. Whenever people ask us what has been the hardest part of our global bicycle adventure, we answer, "pedaling out of our driveway." It was easy to save money compared to working out all the details of moving to our new lifestyle. This wasn't only a vacation where we had to arrange to have our mail held and plants watered. This involved things like juggling our time with ending our jobs, selling our cars and painting the house.

Leaving It All Behind

I came up with a plan that would eventually leave us with only a tent to call home. I feared that this extreme change would be a huge jolt to our mental health. We needed a transitional lifestyle that wasn't yet on the bikes, but with fewer comforts than living in our house. Besides, we had a lot of work to do on the house to prepare it for renters. We wanted renters before we left, so we couldn't stay in our house until the day we left on our bikes. I decided that we would move back into our old and rickety RV as a temporary step between worlds. This was the key to solving the problem.

We started the long process of moving out of the house by having a big garage sale. This wasn't an ordinary garage sale. We were selling almost everything we owned. Things that seemed essential now felt like anchors holding us down. We questioned why we even had a toaster we never used. We had pots that didn't have lids, clothes that were too small and enough extra sheets to supply a small motel. We emptied everything out of the house in two days. Basic essentials and work clothes were set up in the RV, and the rest was placed on the driveway to sell. The prices were ridiculously low. Everything had to go in one short weekend. This drew hordes of people. They were sifting through our things and buying all our possessions.

Our friends and neighbors were concerned; this was the first concrete evidence that we had lost our minds and were serious about leaving. They pleaded with us to "think hard" and reconsider. We were thinking but not the same way they were.

Cindie cried after watching her beloved houseplants, dress shoes, crock-pot and other favorite trinkets vanish from her life. These things must have seemed irreplaceable to her. I had a different outlook on the matter. I felt relieved to lighten the load. We were moving in the right direction. I comforted Cindie, telling her that we could always buy new things but that traveling the world was a once in a lifetime opportunity. Our lives were forever going to be different. It was like taking a giant leap in the dark and hoping to land in a good place.

Finally, everything was sold or given to charity. The last item out of the house was our bed, marking the final conversion to RV living. We stayed parked in the driveway while we prepared our empty house for renters. We cleaned and painted every day after work for a month.

Once the house was ready, we had several property management companies come by and look at it. This was nerve racking. We weren't sure how much monthly rent we could collect. We needed enough to cover the mortgage, 10% property management fees, insurance and a little left over to pay for occasional repairs. We both knew that if we couldn't rent our house for a substantial amount of money that we would have to sell it. I wanted to find a way of keeping our house. I knew from traveling in the past that it's hard not to have a place that I could call home and theoretically return. Most of the property managers told us that our house wouldn't be worth enough in monthly rent to cover our expenses. One company liked our house and believed that it was marketable. They told us that it would be easy to collect enough rent to cover our expenses. We signed a contract, and they took over.

Signing the contract with the property management company meant that we had to move our RV permanently from the driveway. I was teaching at a remote residential school. We parked the RV a few miles from the school. This worked out well in several ways. I was close enough to my job so that I could ride my bike. Besides building my fitness, I was now able to sell my car. Cindie still needed her truck to go to her job. We knew that we would have to sell it at the last possible minute. We never worried about selling the RV because it was disposable. I knew as a last resort that I could always drive it to a junk yard the day before we left.

The other advantage to living in our small RV was that it was free. Our house was now rented and paying for itself. We were still working and could save the money that we normally sent to the mortgage. We did this for several months.

We had been researching touring bikes, travel clothing and camping gear for months. Now that the big job of selling our things and moving out of the house was complete, we were ready to make final decisions and buy equipment. We bought all of our equipment – such as a tent, bike clothing and camp stove – on the internet and sent it to Cindie's work address.

Two Months Before We Left

While we were living in the RV and buying equipment, we had been keeping our plans hidden from people at our work places. Soon, however, boxes were arriving almost daily at Cindie's office because that was now the only physical address we had, and her coworkers were growing suspicious.

My principal and coworkers were confused when I started showing up to work on my mountain bike. They knew that the school was a 45-minute drive from my house. What they didn't know was that we were living in the RV a few miles from the school. When questioned, I told them that I was trying to get back in shape. Rumors were flying around at both of our workplaces. I could only imagine what people were dreaming up to explain things they didn't understand.

Two months before we left, we both submitted resignation letters to our supervisors. I wrote a brief memo announcing when my last day of work would be and that I was quitting because I was leaving on a seven- year around-the-world bike tour. They initially were skeptical; they could not believe that my wild story was true. When Cindie gave notice, her boss took the news better than she expected. He

15

was supportive and helped make the final days of leaving smoother.

Telling all of our friends was much easier than those at our jobs because I had been hinting to them that we were leaving for years. We wrote a group email that we sent to over three hundred friends and both of our families. This letter also committed us to leaving on a specific date. The letter told the world when and where we were going to break free and start living out our dreams.

The Plan: Our Letter –

At this point, we plan to spend the first four weeks meandering around southern Arizona to get our legs strong and break in the gear. Around May 1, 2002, we will cross the US-Mexico border at Douglas and begin the many climbs into the central Mexico highlands. Around July, or so, we want to spend a few weeks going to a Spanish immersion school in Guanajuato, Mexico. The famous velodrome (bicycle race track), where Eddy Merckx set the hour record, is on our list as well. Around October 2002, we will descend out of the Central highlands of Mexico and cross the Guatemalan border in late November, 2002.

We will spend about five months in Central America riding south through Guatemala, El Salvador, Honduras, Nicaragua and Costa Rica until we arrive in Panama around April, 2003. At this time, we plan to visit my family in Indiana and Cindie's family in Connecticut for a month. After our time in the states, we hope to continue either in Colombia or Ecuador around June, 2003. Colombia is a great bike country but not the kind of place you want to visit in a bad year.

If all goes well we will follow the spine of the Andes Mountains south all the way to Southern Chile. We haven't decided whether we want to go all the way to the tip at Terra Del Fuego or not, but around March 2004 we plan on flying to Africa to spend several months riding in the more friendly countries (not in civil war) of that continent.

After Africa, we think that we may want to teach English in Europe. Maybe southern Spain or Greece in September 2004. Athens for the 2004 summer Olympics may be a possibility too. Besides teaching English, we would like to travel around Europe for a year. I am sure we will have to catch a major portion of the Tour De France or we will surely feel like we came to dinner but never really ate.

Things get very sketchy after that, but I can see us flying from Europe to Hong Kong and riding several months in China and eventually meandering south through Asia until we get to Australia. Australia will take about a year to explore. Heading to New Zealand is a requirement that I must accomplish in order to satisfy an agreement that I made with Cindie. You have no idea what other things I had to agree to before she would go on this trip, but she is my trooper and worth every effort.

www.theudora.com/maps

17

Come Join Us

We leave Saturday March 30, 2002. We will have breakfast at the Tecate Grill in downtown Prescott at around 8 a.m. We will be leaving on our adventure from the Prescott Courthouse at 9:30 a.m. I would like to invite anyone who wants to see us off to meet us for breakfast at the Tecate Grill and/or at the Prescott Courthouse to ride with us one last time. I know that this will be impossible for the many out of state recipients of this email and we will have to catch up with you later. For the rest we would like one last grind up the Whitespars together or at least coffee.

We will update our Web page www.downtheroad.org when we can. The site is started but is a shell at this point and will have more content as we travel down the road. We are starting a new email list in order to stay in contact with everyone. If you would like to remain on this list, please reply to this email.

Don't be afraid to write,

Tim and Cindie Travis

The reaction this created was overwhelming. Emotions ran the spectrum from panic to enthusiastic approval.

The Week Before We Left

Cindie had stopped working two weeks before our departure date to visit her twin sister in Alaska. She sold her truck before she left. I stopped working a week before we left and spent time fishing with my brother who came out from Indiana. I needed a place to stay until the last moment while Cindie was in Alaska with her twin sister. I worked out a deal with someone to buy the RV and pick it up the day before our departure. I sold it for a mere $500. This may not sound like much for a RV, but it was more than I expected. It was a much better deal than the $50 that the junk man would have given me for it.

Moving out of our RV was a big job but much easier than moving out of the house. Everything was on a smaller scale. Two nights before we left I unloaded the RV in front of Cindie's office. The entire contents of the RV went to three different piles: to be loaded on our bikes; to go to charity; to the dumpster. I stayed up the entire night to complete this in time for the buyer to pick up the RV at the agreed time.

The last thing I removed was my homemade calendar. It was only a single piece of paper now. I sat down and contemplated what this final page meant to me. I had made this calendar almost three years before and patiently waited for this moment. We had sacrificed and saved all this time. I no longer needed my calendar. Time was up. I had won the waiting game. I slowly folded it into a paper airplane and threw it to freedom. It was my own private victory celebration.

After Cindie returned from Alaska we no longer owned motor vehicles. Standing in Cindie's office, we both noticed that we didn't have any keys on our key rings. The key to our house was now with the property manager, our work keys were returned and the car keys were given to the new owners. It was a strange feeling. We were free of this expense and responsibility. We were now down to the bare minimum.

The Night Before We Left

The night before we left was filled with the one last job to be completed before we earned our freedom. We had to take the pile of gear and food on the floor of Cindie's office and somehow load it on our two bicycles. This required me to stay up for my second all-nighter in a row. Even though we had prepared and planned for years, we still felt as if we weren't ready. It was the first time that we completely packed our bikes. It quickly became evident that not everything on the floor could come along. We were asking ourselves what we could spend the next several years without. We asked each other "Is this all I get to cook with? "Do you think that I can live with fewer clothes?"

The amount of nonperishable food that had come out of the RV was staggering. We had fallen short of eating the canned food such as peas and soup. We came up with a quick solution to deal with it. We had it mailed to a town in Arizona (Portal) near the Mexican border. As one last going away gift, Cindie's boss picked up the tab for mailing the boxes to us. We planned to pick it up in several weeks. Even though we stayed up all night, we had to rush at the end. The last hour was spent frantically cramming gear into our bags and indiscriminately tying things onto rear racks. We looked like amateurs.

Cindie packing the night before we left.

2 Arizona: Freedom at Last!

(March 30 – May 12, 2002)

Our new bikes could have set a record for weight. Instead of leaving it all behind it was as if we were bringing it all with us. The three-block ride to the restaurant was almost impossible because of a steep hill. In addition to over full panniers, (saddlebags), I had strapped our camp chairs, tent and walking shoes on to the back of my bike. My rear pannier had a dozen cans of food in each bag and included all our pots and pans. Cindie's panniers were also full, and she had our sleeping bags strapped on the back. Our bikes were awkward; like a stranger that we just met. There was a look of fear on Cindie's face.

When we rolled our bikes into the restaurant, we received a standing ovation from fifty of our friends. Cindie was brought to tears while I wasn't sure why they were applauding. I guess it was because we had finally made it. We had spent all of our time and effort preparing to leave and never thought about the emotions we would face when we actually left. We felt uprooted; we were starting something big and ending something familiar at the same time.

We pushed our bikes into the restaurant and set them against the wall. Everyone congregated around and had a contest to see who could pick up my bike. No one could. Cindie's stomach was in a knot, and I had no appetite. We nervously ate and wondered what the day would bring. Sadly, we felt as if we were unable to visit with everyone. It would have been nice to have a long conversation with each one of them. We talked to as many friends as we could, and suddenly it was time to go to the courthouse, the starting point of our journey.

At the courthouse, even more people arrived. I hid my sadness behind my sunglasses the best I could while Cindie was overwhelmed with emotion. Suddenly I realized the good things I was leaving behind. Prescott, Arizona was a great place to live. This was the big moment, and I had trouble finding the right words to say. I thanked everybody for seeing us off and asked them to stay in contact through email. We climbed on our bikes for what seemed the first time in our lives and started down the longest road we would ever ride. This road we began to call home.

Once we were rolling, the true test of my grand plan confronted us. The first six miles (ten kilometers) out of Prescott climb over a mountain pass. Although we were very familiar with this road, it felt physically impossible on such heavy bikes. Combine this with the fact that there hadn't been enough time to exercise while we prepared to leave therefore, we were out of shape.

My bike was poorly packed, unbalanced, and difficult to steer. It was the heaviest load I have ever pedaled. Cindie

Our bikes loaded to the maximum on the first day.

had difficulty keeping her bicycle in a straight line. We both had limited control and would swerve from side to side. The fifteen people riding with us politely kept his or her distance because they became concerned for our safety. Someone suggested that we camp close to town, have a feast to lighten our load and ask for our jobs back on Monday morning.

As we rode further out of town, they turned around one by one. All the paths they were taking led back to the same place and comfortable lives. Our road led somewhere else, a place that we had only seen on maps and in guidebooks; it was the road that had no end. We parted with the last of our escort after a couple of hours, and then there were two.

Ten miles (sixteen kilometers) from our destination, I pushed my bike onto the dirt and laid down to rest in the shade. I hadn't slept in 48 hours. As I was getting ready to ride the last few miles to Yarnell, I noticed goat heads on my jersey. Goat heads are nature's imitation of the sharp metal spikes that the police throw under fleeing car tires. They grow in the high desert and are feared by all cyclists. Sure enough when I inspected my tires, I found one pushed in deep. When I pulled it out, I heard the familiar hissing sound indicating our first flat tire only hours after we started. We were tired from our first real athletic effort in months and now we had to pull everything off my bike and fix my flat. I had no idea where anything was, such as tubes and the necessary tools. Cindie thought that this unfortunate event should be documented, and her daily journal began. From that day on, Cindie kept a journal describing the daily events during our years on the road. All of her daily journals can be found on our Web site www.downtheroad.org. Around 5:00 p.m. we made it to Yarnell and made our first free camp on an empty plot of land. We went to bed early and slept hard for twelve hours.

First Day of the Rest of Our Lives

We woke up in the morning with absolutely nothing on our schedule. We didn't have meetings to attend, bills to pay, jobs to go to or friends to meet. Even though by car we were only an hour away from where we had started, I felt like we were in another world. Something magical had happened during the night. We had crossed over to the other side. It was the first completely free day of our lives. This was the feeling that I had dreamed about for so long. We had sacrificed and worked hard to make it happen, but now it was here. A giant weight of stress and worry was lifted from our shoulders. There isn't anything else like it. It can only be described as complete FREEDOM!

We sat in our new camp chairs and slowly made breakfast on our new stove. We didn't think about this at the time, but this would be the last time everything we owned was

Our first campsite in Yarnell, Arizona.

new. We had all the time in the world. This was unfamiliar to us. We watched the birds slowly float through the morning air. We didn't know what to say to each other. We felt as if talking about our new found freedom would make the feeling somehow disappear. It was early afternoon before we climbed back on the bikes.

As we cycled along the desert floor, we developed a saying that we repeated to each other often when the road turned up or the wind blew in our face. "At least we get to ride today." That describes what our new freedom first meant to us. We could ride as much as we wanted. In the months and years that followed, our freedom took on a more complicated meaning.

All this bike riding had other advantages. In Tucson, I weighed myself, and I had lost ten pounds in the first week. Cindie had lost a proportional amount of weight as well. Both our physical and mental health improved. The negative effect that stressful lives and jobs had placed on our health wasn't noticed until it was gone. Once it was removed, we slept better, ate less and were much happier.

After visiting friends in Tucson, we turned off the paved road and rode deep into the national forest. This marked our first dirt road and another test. The bumpy road shook our bikes, and I seriously thought that our gear couldn't take it. I especially worried about the computer in my rear pannier. Fortunately, nothing broke, but several bolts needed to be tightened on the bikes. After a pleasant night of camping under the stars, we found pavement again. Neither of us was sure that we actually liked dirt roads, but at least we knew we could do it.

We rode south passed Tucson and Green Valley until we approached the Mexican border. Our plan was to spend more time in Arizona in familiar surroundings to become used to our new equipment and lifestyle. We knew the language and culture in Arizona. Mexico would add another dimension to life on a bike. We turned north again to visit more of our own country.

We camped at Parker Canyon Lake for two nights. We didn't want to pay for the campground so we rode around to the opposite side of the lake and made a free camp. On this seldom-visited side, we came across an illegal immigrant family hiding in the shade. The family included a one-year-old child and her mother who was seven months pregnant. They looked tired and dirty like they had been on the road for a long time. They were obviously hiding out during the day and walking all night. Our interaction with them was tense, but non-confrontational. They didn't want us to tell the border patrol, and I didn't want them to think we were any kind of threat. Anyone in the situation of being illegal has the potential of being dangerous. We didn't intend to tell the authorities. They were going into our country looking for a better life, and we were going into their country seeking the same. For months after this, Cindie talked about how tough the pregnant mother was.

Tombstone, Arizona

We had both been to Tombstone. Several movies about Wyatt Earp, Doc Holiday and the legendary shoot out at the OK Corral have made this town famous. Tombstone is a tourist destination and expensive. The OK Corral has walls completely around it to prevent tourists from looking inside. It costs $3 to get in and listen to a recording depicting the famous event. The old courthouse cost $2.50 to enter and was probably worth it, but we were on the cheap, so we had to look elsewhere.

At the Tombstone Tourist office, I asked, "What can you see for free around here?" We were directed to the Tombstone Epitaph, which was the original newspaper in town and is Arizona's oldest running newspaper. As their saying goes, "Every Tombstone needs an Epitaph." It cost nothing to roam around the old printing presses and antique office equipment.

We looked at several different printing presses representing technological advances through the years. The first printing press was that - a press. The type is set and a piece of paper is placed under it. Next, the printer cranked the

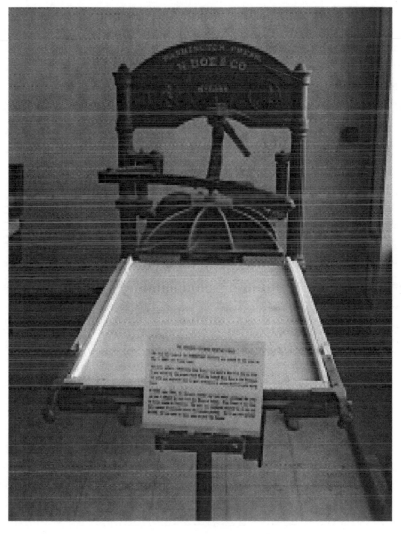

Early Printing Press.

inked metal plate down over the paper. It must have taken a long time for each edition to be printed. The paper came out weekly, was passed around to dozens of people, and ended up on a distant ranch or mining camp - months old and worn out. As a teacher, I wonder how many kids and adults learned to read from obituaries and exaggerated accounts of stage robberies in this newspaper.

Tombstone is on the road between Sierra Vista and several ghost towns in the area. It was never on our list of places to visit, and we could have easily passed through, but when you travel by bike, you always need things like food, water and ice cream.

A couple hours out of Tombstone, on a seldom-used dirt road, we camped for the night in the open desert. There were dozens of ghost towns melting into the ground nearby. In the early morning light, we saw a slow moving Border Patrol airplane circling overhead. I didn't want them to think we were lost, so I gave the pilot a thumbs up. He eventually left. Later that morning we rode past a uniformed man in a border patrol truck. We waved at each other. I thought that he might want to stop us and check our ID; however, we were riding south which wouldn't be normal for illegal aliens.

We visited several ghost towns along our remote dirt road from Tombstone to Chiricahua. This was once the main route in the area and we imagined wagon trains and cattle drives beside us. These ghost towns were some of the best historical sites we found with no gatekeeper charging admission or tacky gift shops. They were only old frontier towns that lost their economic reasons for existing, but the structures and stories still cling to life. One of our favorites was Gleason. There we noticed an old looking graveyard and we had to dismount and investigate closer. Some of the graves were from the 1800's. The epitaphs revealed only hints of the wild lives that were short- lived, but are now gone. We were in the forgotten Wild West.

Arizona: Freedom at Last!

Cindie on the dirt road from Tombstone to Chiricahua.

Adobe ruins near Gleason Arizona.

Tim Travis

Chiricahua National Monument

Riding with the wind at our backs made crossing the desert fun. The weather was a pleasant 70° Fahrenheit (21° Celsius), the air was dry and dusty; it felt good to be gliding down the road. We completed a long sixty miles (ninety-six kilometers) to the Chiricahua National Monument. Even with the help of the wind, we arrived at the park entrance gate tired and hungry. The park official informed us that the only campground in the Park was full and we would have to ride several miles uphill on a dirt road to camp. This would take several hours; it was late, and we were already tired. I noticed that there was a small water cooler in the guardhouse. I pulled out our 2.6-gallon (ten liter) water bag and asked the Park Official if she could fill it. In Arizona, it's illegal to refuse someone water. She didn't have enough water in her small cooler to fill my water bag. She told us that there was a water faucet a half mile inside the park. We

Rhyolite columns, Chiricahua National Monument, Arizona.

rode in and didn't ride back out for three days. Once inside the park, we found a hidden place to camp. We laid the bikes down in the brush and didn't put up the tent. First thing in the morning, we hopped on our still loaded bikes and went to the nearest picnic area for morning coffee and breakfast. We rode to the park campground and moved into a space as someone was leaving.

In Chiricahua National Monument, we went on our first day hike of the trip. In time, we would seek more hiking opportunities as a diversion from pedaling. A shuttle drove us to the top of the mountain and a wonderful trail descended back to the campground. The scenery was superb: rhyolite rock pillars wind blown into different formations were all along the trail while the panoramic view included mountaintop vistas.

From Chiricahua National Monument, we steadily rode into the national forest on a steep dirt road. It took us several hours to reach the place where the park ranger had told us that we could camp when we first arrived. We camped alone and found a spring that provided water for cleaning up. The next day we continued to ride up towards the pass. Our prize was Onion Pass and our first altitude record at 7,600 feet (2,318 meters). At the time, this was a big deal to us. It meant that we were becoming more fit. In the future, we would climb much higher in the Sierra Madre Mountains in central Mexico. The descent to Portal, Arizona was more difficult than the climb. We were learning that our loaded touring bikes handled differently on steep dirt descents compared to our unloaded mountain bikes that we had ridden in Prescott. By the time we reached Portal, AZ, we had gone nearly a week without even the smallest of stores to buy food. We ate the last of the canned food from the RV that we had stuffed into my bike three weeks earlier in Prescott.

Portal, Arizona

Portal, Arizona is close to paradise. We stayed for three weeks, including a six-day backpacking trip in the nearby Chiricahua Mountains. Portal is known internationally as a bird watching and naturalist area. The density and variety of wildlife is unique.

Portal sits at the end of a long lush canyon with a year round creek that draws its water from the high Chiricahua Mountains to the west. To the east is the state of New Mexico and to the south is the Chihuahua desert that stretches far south into Mexico.

The first birders we met were Frank and Robin from Berkeley, California. They came to Portal as often as they could. In their camping van they had a library of books for identifying birds, plants, rocks and mammals. We camped next to them for a week. I have never been around bird watchers or "Birders" as they often call themselves. The only required equipment is high quality binoculars, field guide-books for bird identification and an outrageous floppy hat. Some have cameras, but this wasn't a requirement. Many of the people we met in Portal were world renowned in natural-ist circles. Many of them had written well-known books in their specific field of expertise. I liked their priorities.

Birders had interesting habits. You can guess that they walked around during the day with their binoculars looking at various birds and identifying them in their field books. We also participated in this activity for hours. The activity that was the oddest to me was owling. Owling is the art of walking in the woods at dusk and well after dark to look for owls. For this, you can leave your floppy sun hat behind, but you do need a flashlight. We went several times with locals and with Frank and Robin. When we heard an owl making its "who" or "hoot" noise, we closed in and figured out what branch it was on. This was no easy task because it was dark.

Arizona: Freedom at Last!

Our campsite in Portal, Arizona.

Cindie birding with Frank and Robin.

Once we found and identified the owl, one person held the light on the owl while everyone else looked in his or her binoculars. When Frank and Robin saw us looking through our miniature travel binoculars, they insisted that we use their much more powerful binoculars. One night while we were looking for the little (6-inch, 15 centimeters, high) Elf Owl, a van load of people parked and silently got out with their lights (off) and binoculars around their neck. Without saying a word, they stood in the darkness listening for a specific owl. After a few moments, they walked on without making a sound.

We saw other animals in the Portal area that I had never seen before: many kinds of hummingbirds, screech owl, great horned owl, elf owl, ring-tailed cat (who ate my fig newtons), skunk (who ate my oatmeal), coati, gray fox, deer, javalina, and a phantom black bear.

Chiricahua Mountains Trek

While in Portal, we stored our bikes with a local resident and enjoyed a 6-day backpacking trip. We had always dreamed of backpacking in the Chiricahuas, which are remote, high in altitude and have many trails. These mountains look more like parts of Colorado rather than the surrounding desert. This isn't what people typically expect southern Arizona to look like. These pine-covered mountains are called "Sky Islands" because of their micro climate. They have high alpine vegetation and wildlife. In the late 1800s, the Apache Indians lived in these sky islands and used the rugged terrain to hide from US troops chasing them.

During our backpack trip, we visited a known camp of the great Apache Chief Victorio. We went on a long day hike to Buena Vista Peak and then down to a flat meadow with a running spring where Victorio's band had camped and hidden from the US Army several times. Despite the recent drought, the spring was trickling out water. This was the perfect place to hide hundreds of warriors and families in

34

Victorio's band. The US Army could have been spotted from a nearby peak hours before they arrived. Even if they had marched up the hill, they would have had a hard time finding this hidden meadow. The Apache had taken advantage of the rugged terrain and set a trap. The soldiers, marching up the 3000-foot (915 meters) trail, would have been in no condition to take on Apache Warriors who were rested and attacking from high cliffs. We had lunch near the meadow as we imagined these events.

Dave, a local wildlife artist, let us camp in his yard for a few days after our backpacking trip. We enjoyed his yard of bird feeders and the various animals that came to visit. One night while sleeping under the stars in Dave's yard, a bear came to dine on the sugar water in the numerous hummingbird feeders. The feeders were nine feet (2.75 meters) in the air; however, the bear didn't have a problem reaching them. Dave chased the bear out of the yard, and we stayed awake the rest of the night waiting for the bear to return.

Riding from Portal to Douglas, Arizona and the Mexican border took two days. It was only sixty-one miles (98 kilometers), but a dust storm and a strong headwind of about thirty miles per hour (mph) (forty-eight kilometers per hour kph) forced us to take refuge. The only shelter from the wind we could find to spend the night was a roadside monument to the final place the great Apache medicine man, Geronimo, surrendered. We used a picnic table as a block for the stinging wind and sand.

That night we didn't pitch our tent. The wind would have destroyed it. We were only twenty miles (thirty-two kilometers) north of the USA/Mexican border. We heard that the US Border Patrol catches ten thousand illegal immigrants a year in this valley. This is estimated to be only 10% of the total people crossing. I stayed awake all night after I heard people walking by and whispering in Spanish.

Monument to Geronimo's final surrender, and where we spent the night.

The next day on the road to Douglas a rancher in his pickup truck stopped next to us and asked us if we wanted a can of pop from his cooler. We accepted. He introduced himself as Randy and told us that he had lived in this area his whole life. When we told him where we had camped the previous night, he asked if we had trouble with illegals. I told him no, but we had heard many people walking by us. He said that the illegals often cut his irrigation lines to get a drink of water and in the process drained the ten thousand gallon (37,800 liters) water tank. This caused major problems for his ranching business because the lack of water regularly kills a substantial percentage of his herd. He went on to explain his views of how illegal immigrants take jobs and lower wages. I kept asking if there was a way to solve this problem so that conditions improved on both sides of the border. He had no answer.

Arizona: Freedom At Last!

We rode into Douglas, Arizona and found the cheapest hotel room near the border for our last nights in Arizona. The small border cities of Douglas, Arizona and Agua Prieta, Mexico have many advantages for a bicycle tourist. They are both smaller than the other border crossings, and this makes navigation and traffic much easier. We shopped in familiar American stores in Douglas. We weren't sure what would be available in Mexico. We also used up the last of our $0.06 a minute calling card to contact our families. We knew that calling from Mexico would cost much more, and we would be reduced to using email.

I connected our laptop computer to the internet using our calling card and the telephone line in our hotel room. I updated our Web site with dozens of pictures and Cindie's daily journal. The Web site was receiving an average of five visitors a day. We didn't expect more because it was only meant for friends and family. By placing our files on the Web site, they were backed up if our computer was broken or stolen. We sent an email to our list that explained what we had been doing in Arizona and our general plans in Northern Mexico. Our email list contained only a few recipients. We personally knew them all. At the time I couldn't have possibly imagined how big and busy our Web site would become.

I had no idea how I was going to connect our computer to the internet once we crossed the border. I knew from previous trips to Mexico that telephones didn't exist in cheap hotel rooms. This important detail would need to be figured out along the way.

In these border towns, it was clear what items are cheap in each country. On the USA side, Mexican citizens were streaming out of large department stores with TV's, personal computers and other consumer electronics. High taxes in Mexico make these items expensive. Those with cars also filled up on the much cheaper and cleaner American gasoline.

US citizens cross into Mexico to buy prescription drugs that are several times cheaper. A retired American woman told us that the exact same asthma inhaler and heart medicine, made in the USA, is much cheaper in Mexico. She said that she went to Mexico every six months to stock up on her prescription drugs. This greatly improved her living standards on her fixed income. Americans also go to Mexico to buy cheaper American-brand cigarettes and Mexican-made hard alcohol. The trade between the two countries is brisk.

Our last night in the USA was spent wondering what dangers and adventures were waiting for us south of the border. We wondered if there were bandits hiding in the hills and parasites lurking in restaurants.

Tim and Cindie Travis ready to roll, photo taken by Dave Utterback.

3 Mexico: Crossing Over

(May 13 – May 31, 2002)

We had received several warnings from concerned friends and family about our plan to ride our bicycles through Mexico. Some went as far as to say that we would be killed for our bikes before our first week was over.

We entered Mexico on May 13, 2002, two and a half months after we started our trip. For us, there was no looking back; we had to cross the border. Travelers are ruled by their curiosity.

We assumed that the Mexican side of the border would be very much like the U.S. side of the border. After all, they were only yards (meters) apart. We expected a transition time so we could gradually get use to a different culture.

Those were bad assumptions.

Cindie at the US-Mexico border.

English disappeared completely and was replaced by Spanish. We couldn't understand the signs or the people. People looked at us, pointed and spoke, but we didn't know what they were saying. Colorful Mexican pesos with unknown presidents and values replaced our familiar green dollar bills. Kilometers replaced miles while Celsius replaced Fahrenheit. Food was regularly cooked in the streets on wheeled carts with a wide variety of new smells and shapes.

Agua Prieta isn't an ordinary Mexican city; it's a border town. Thousands of Latin Americans from all points south arrive here and spend several days arranging to cross illegally into the USA. People in transit were hanging around on every street corner. They yelled at us the English words they knew: "come here, good-bye." The two-lane road out of town was busy and narrow. There were double trailer trucks that made the exhaust-belching beast twice as long. The shoulder of this narrow road consisted of a small cliff that ended in spent diapers and other nasty smelling trash.

On the outskirts of town at a military checkpoint, the Mexican soldiers questioned us. One of them spoke English. They asked us several unimportant questions concerning our travels. They must have been bored with searching vehicles for guns and drugs. They told us that it was 159 kilometers (99 miles) before the next town or water source. That information was useful, but we already anticipated it from looking at our maps. We were carrying an extra five gallons (nineteen liters) of water and food for a week.

Four miles after the checkpoint, a van with at least four men drove slowly past us; they were staring at us more than the average. A few minutes later, we saw the van parked on a small hill next to the road. Traffic was frequent, and several vehicles passed us as we approached. When we were near, I heard a man yell the Spanish word for "tools" and "help" at us. He was waving a large wrench and obviously wanted us to stop.

Why was only one man visible? The others would surely be investigating under the hood. I didn't see them. Why had this man watched several cars go by, including a welding truck full of tools, and not asked them for help? How did a van that quit running park on top of a hill and not on the side of the road? The pieces weren't fitting together.

The border area is known for foul play. If we stopped to help, they could easily overpower and drag us behind the hill out of sight of the road. I trusted my instincts and gave Cindie our hand signal to speed up. As we passed the man pleaded with me to stop and help fix his van. I couldn't understand his words entirely, but his tone made me feel guilty for not being a Good Samaritan.

On reflection, I can't be positive about the intentions of the men in the van, but the evidence was against them. As time passed and I gained more experience on the road, they grew more and more guilty. I learned to trust my instincts; especially near international borders. In the end, our instincts are all that any of us can rely on.

It was 94 miles (150 kilometers) to the next town, but we had the large double trucks to keep us company. We crossed over two mountain passes including the continental divide. We encountered a forest fire along the road. To my surprise, the police waved us through and we rode right next to the flames.

The second night we found a small narrow canyon near the pass of a mountain chain. We were tired and went about making a tentless camp because the weather was good, and we didn't want to be seen from the road. After setting up I looked in a nearby arroyo (dry creekbed) for water to take a shower. I didn't find any water, but I did find a staging area where people prepared to cross the border illegally. Lying on the ground was a pile of backpacks with kid's clothes and toys. I even saw several stuffed animals. This upset me very

A double trailer truck.

much. These kids probably didn't have much to begin with and had parted with their only toys to travel light.

After the three-day desert crossing, we arrived in Janos to find a dry dusty place and a major truck stop between Mexico City and Tijuana. The hotel owner told us truck drivers take drugs to stay awake for the four-day drive between the two cities. We were now nervous about sharing the road with sleepy truckers. We rented our first hotel room in Latin America. Toilets in Latin America couldn't handle paper so a trash can nearby held it. This trash can ranged from empty and clean to full and disgusting. The acceptable noise level of neighbors was unrestricted. Televisions were turned all the way up the entire night while the occupants slept soundly. Not all aspects of this new culture were inviting.

The next day we had a pleasant ride through irrigated cornfields on a gently rolling road. Seeing all the tractors and corn reminded me of growing up in Indiana. Shortly after a roadside lunch of peanut butter and tortillas, we rolled into Nuevos Casa Grande.

Paquime Ruins Casas Grandes, Mexico

Nuevos Casa Grande was the first town outside the border zone that we visited, and the town was much more relaxed. While resting in Nuevos Casa Grande for a few days, we took a day trip to the Paquime Ruins. The ruins were occupied from 900 to 1340 A.D., and as many as ten thousand people lived there. The Paquimes built a complex web of canals with cisterns to irrigate their crops in this arid environment. They also built adobe cages to raise Macaws; their feathers were used for ceremonial purposes. We found that the adjacent interpretive center was modern and informative.

A few miles south of Nuevo Casa Grande, the semi trucks took a different route to Mexico City, and our riding conditions improved immensely. We left the desert behind and

Paquime ruins.

climbed a mountain for twenty miles (thirty-two kilometers). At the top was a cool plateau of pine trees, cornfields and apple orchards.

The Mexicans in this rural farming area had a much slower pace of life compared to their urban counterparts. Everyone was all smiles and wanted to talk to us and even take us into their homes. Our Spanish was minimal, but the locals didn't care. We constantly had our Spanish – English dictionary out and struggled through every interaction. Mexicans are extremely patient and helped us learn their language. Their constant encouragement showed us that they appreciated our effort to speak their language.

The night before we planned to reach Cuauhtemoc, we were looking for a place to camp in a large commercial apple orchard. Cindie asked a worker tinkering with an irrigation pump if we could camp in the orchard.

He said, "Senior Vicente" and pointed at a group of men welding underneath an old tractor. We rode over to the group of men and asked for Senior Vicente. The man supervising told us he was Senior Vicente. We were all smiles, which I believe communicates more than any language can. Cindie knew the word for "camping" and repeated it while pointing into the field. He looked puzzled and said several things in Spanish, which we didn't understand. I pointed at the tent and sleeping bags strapped to the back of our bikes. He still didn't understand. He then spoke to one of his workers, warmly shook my hand, and gave a nervous chuckle.

The worker motioned for us to follow him. We were led to the apple processing factory that was empty and idle outside of harvest time. This man tried to ask us many questions, but we didn't understand. I guessed that one of his questions was "Where are you from?" I answered, "The United States" and then "Arizona." He was excited to hear this. Next, he told us something in a long sentence, but all I caught was the word brother and Phoenix, Arizona. I think he was tell-

Cindie with our visitors in the apple factory.

ing us that he had a brother in Phoenix. I understood him when he asked if we came all of that way on bicycles. Well, I understood "on bicycle." I would have liked to have been able to talk with him more, but the language barrier made it impossible. I did understand through hand motions that we could sleep in the factory and no one would bother us. He understood that we were traveling by bicycles and that we were harmless.

We laid out our ground cloth, camping mattress and sleeping bags. When the workday was over everyone went home. We thought we were alone and pulled out our computer to move pictures from our digital camera to the hard drive. The light from the computer must have been easy to see in the darkness because we soon had visitors. A woman and her young children came in and sat down. The kids were interested in our computer. Not knowing what else to do I gave them a slide show of all of the pictures we had taken since the day we had left.

45

They became excited when viewing the pictures from northern Mexico. Eventually they recognized the scenes in the pictures because they were taken recently. Through the eye of my camera, they saw what we saw: a beautiful landscape worthy of taking photos.

Even though we didn't speak a common language, a lot of interaction and communication took place on that warehouse floor. I learned that our computer could be a tool to bridge cultures. It's said that, "A picture is worth a thousand words," and I believe these words are always in the first language of the viewer. From this point on, when conditions were right, I would give slide shows on our computer. These slide shows contained a few pictures of us, but I concentrated on places near the viewer's home. This always instilled pride in the viewers and produced a positive reaction. All people should think that the place where they live is as picturesque as any other place on earth.

In the morning, the kids brought us breakfast and sat with us until their mother told them that they were going to be late to school. I didn't understand her words, but a child's reality around the world is surprisingly similar.

We said good-bye to the workers who were welding another tractor. We left them with hearty handshakes and a new understanding of their neighbors to the North. We learned that communication would be possible no matter what corner of the globe we find ourselves.

Back on the road, it was windy again. It was the fifth day in a row that we were greeted by a headwind, a wind blowing directly in our faces. The headwind was strong and constant; this requires an effort like climbing a never-ending hill. Like a major foe, it stalked us in the highlands of Chihuahua. Everyday it stole from us and tried to convince us to turn around and coast back north. The howling noise made conversation between us and with locals difficult. The headwind grew worse as we rode south and made life miserable. We promised each other that if it didn't stop by the time we reached Cuauhtemoc, we would catch a bus. I hoped that the wind would be blowing in a different direction further south.

When we reached the village of Bachiniva, we sat in the plaza sheltered from the wind. Even though we weren't far from the apple factory, it had taken hours to ride here because of wind. We must have looked as if we needed help because when we asked about a restaurant we were invited into an elderly woman's kitchen. Even though we understood little of what they said the food and the company were wonderful. It was all women and me. I felt as if I was at a tea party. We had authentic homemade chili rellenos for breakfast. Cindie was shown recipes and various Mexican delicacies being prepared. They wanted her to know how real Mexican food looked and tasted. When we were done eating one of the women held a key in the air and said it was to the old church in town. We were taken on a tour of an old

Tim in the kitchen with our hosts.

church built in the times of the Spanish. From the bell tower we could see the entire village and far off on the high plain.

After breakfast, we struggled against the wind again. It was miserable to work so hard on a perfectly flat road and go so slow. We stopped in Obregon for a long rest out of the wind. We read in our guidebook that Mennonites lived in the area. The Mennonites (German farmers) migrated here in the 1920s from Europe, the United States and Canada to escape persecution for their religious beliefs. They lived a primitive farming lifestyle with the men wearing coveralls and the women wearing Victorian style dresses and large bonnets. They were prosperous people who spoke an old German dialect and Spanish. I tried to interact with them but didn't get far. They lived in a closed society, and it was difficult to break the ice.

After a lunch of tacos we took to the road with Cuauhtemoc as our destination. The wind had other plans for us. It did its dirty work and slowed us to a fast walk. We found ourselves (drained) several hours away from Cuauhtemoc, and it was growing dark. We were looking for places to camp, but this was a populated agriculture area with no place to hide. We saw a sign for an RV park and pulled in for a look at the first and last RV Park in Latin America. We hadn't seen a single RV on the road. The RV Park was empty and closed, and there was no one to ask permission to camp. We couldn't go any further and made camp on the office back porch. Before we could pitch the tent a truck pulled in with its headlight directly on us. We thought the worst and prepared to be thrown out. The driver told us that the RV Park was closed. When the man saw us nervously struggling with our dictionary to find the Spanish word for "tired" he asked us in German if we spoke German. When he saw our confusion he switched to clear English. He was Peter, a tall blond Mennonite and owner of the RV Park.

Cindie explained that we were traveling on bicycles, were tired from fighting the wind all day and then asked if we could please camp. Peter was friendly and told us that the wind would make setting up our tent difficult and that we could stay in the common room of the RV Park. He unlocked the door and talked with us while we laid our pads and sleeping bags down. The RV Park was open during the winter when it was full of retirees from Canada and the USA. In the off-season, the park was empty, and Peter drove a dump truck for work.

In the morning, Peter was already gone in his truck when we left. It would have been nice to say good-bye and offer him money for the night. We battled the wind one last day to reach Cuauhtemoc.

Cuauhtemoc, Chihuahua

Riding into Cuauhtemoc was both frightening and confusing. It was our first large Mexican city. We learned that traffic behavior in the cities is much different from the country roads and villages. Mexican country roads and traffic are similar to the back roads in the USA. People are courteous, and there is space on the road for everyone. City traffic in Mexico has a much different culture compared to the city riding we were used to in the USA. Lane markings are ignored, stoplights are merely suggestions and drivers prefer their horns to their brakes. The constant honking is unnerving while weaving through traffic on a bicycle. We avoided as much of it as possible and dismounted as soon as we found the hotel zone.

In Cuauhtemoc we were eager to connect our computer to the internet but not sure how. We found a computer store that did repairs and installed office networks. On the wall were several Microsoft Certifications and diplomas from various technological institutes. Adjacent to the technical department was an internet cafe where Cindie surfed on a high-speed connection for US$1 an hour while I talked to the technicians. To my surprise, the head technician spoke some English. I showed him our computer and asked if it could be connected to the internet as we traveled around the world. I thought that he would use a telephone line. He explained to me that it would be easier to connect to their network. The telephone wasn't the best solution because different parts of the world use different phone jacks, currents and systems. He explained that Microsoft networks and network cables are universal. I received a quick lesson in unplugging the network cable from a computer in an internet cafe and plugging it into the network port on my computer. Numerous settings had to be copied from the original computer to my computer. These settings were in Spanish on their computer and English on mine. The technician worked fast, and I was unable to follow along completely. This would take time and practice to learn. Once I was connected, I had a fast broad-

Plaza in Cuauhtemoc.

band connection. This was a solution to a big problem and a new challenge at the same time.

Once I was connected, I published several megabytes of photos and Cindie's journal to our Web site. Receiving email was just as easy. We had been in Mexico for two weeks without contact with concerned friends and family. Those who had predicted that we would be robbed or killed in Mexico wrote heartfelt emails pleading for us to return to the USA. Some, picturing us penniless and in a dark Mexican police station, even had a hint of "I told you so." We sent a group mail to everyone on our slowly growing email list explaining that we were fine and that Mexico became safe and friendly once we broke free of the border zone.

Copper Canyon

In Cuauhtemoc, we took a break from riding and set off to see the famous Barranca del Cobre, or Copper Canyon. We left our bikes behind in our hotel room and opted for the train that snaked into the canyon. The building of this train is one of the great engineering marvels on the continent.

We had to choose between two classes of trains. The Primavera (first) Class was for tourists to sit in plush dining cars while checking out the abundant scenery. Segunda (second) Class was half the price of Primavera but slower and with older cars. Locals mostly used this train as transportation.

The Primavera Class train came rolling up to the platform where we were standing. An employee of the railroad asked us if we wanted it to stop and was astounded when we told him that we wanted Segunda Class. We were the only non-Hispanic people around and the only ones he asked about the Primavera train. Because no one was getting on the Primavera train, he waved it on. The Mexicans around us were surprised when the train passed, and we happily waited for the Segundo class train.

Copper Canyon.

Copper Canyon train.

Once on the train we couldn't believe how nice it was. "This is the cheap train" we kept saying to ourselves. This wasn't at all a "chicken bus" kind of place. The seats were big and had tons of legroom. Everyone was well dressed; we were the only ones in T-shirts and sandals. The Mexicans quickly went to sleep. They had probably been on this train dozens of times, and Mexicans are masters of sleeping on public transportation. We were wide-eyed and taking pictures.

The scenery that rolled by was familiar to us at first. We had spent the previous weeks bicycling through this part of Mexico. We saw adobe houses where the pace of life looked comfortable and slow. Occasionally, we saw men on horseback trotting to town to pick up something from the village store. They rode easily as if they had ridden all of their lives. Even though these people see trains come by every day, they still gathered on the porch to wave at us as the train passed.

When we came closer to the canyon we saw the Tarahumara, an indigenous group that lives in the area. They inhabit the canyon and the pine covered rim country and still practice a traditional way of life. This is in part because

Adobe house.

the rugged canyons keep them isolated from mainstream Mexico. The Tarahumara number over fifty thousand, and some migrate out of the canyons up into the cooler plateau in the summer to escape the heat. Unlike the Mexican families waving from their porches, the Tarahumara were out of sight when the train passed. They have a reputation for being shy and distant.

When the train rolled up to our stop at Divisidero, everyone got off. This was the only place that people on the train could walk around, stretch their legs, and buy something to eat. We were bombarded with the now familiar smells of chili rellenos, tacos and other local favorites. We also met our first non-Mexican tourist, Jim, since we had crossed the border.

Jim was from Liverpool, England but had been living and traveling in foreign countries for the past several years. He traveled to every corner of the globe and was a wealth of information about the places that we intended to visit over the next several years. His current journey was from South America to Alaska, and he was in his eighteenth month of traveling.

After we gulped in the immense view of Copper Canyon, we started thinking about a place to spend the night. We had left our tent and other camping equipment behind in Cuauhtemoc, so we had to find a hotel. We hitched a ride with Jim into a village not far from the Divisidero train station.

From our hotel room, we hiked along a Tarahumara footpath to several different viewpoints. Unfortunately, this canyon has a similar problem as Arizona's Grand Canyon: pictures don't do it justice. At one viewpoint there was a rickety ladder that plunged into the depths of the canyon. We never saw where the ladder started and we all agreed that descending it would be dangerous. Just as we made this agreement, a Tarahumara man appearing to be sixty years old came up the ladder carrying heavy bags. He wasn't even out of breath. Without saying a word, he walked at a brisk pace into the pines. We were still too scared to go down the ladder.

We walked back to our room, spent the night, and then walked back to the train station the next day. The train ride back to Cuauhtemoc was as enjoyable as the ride out.

Because of the constant wind, Cindie and I honored our promise to each other to take the bus south. We rode the bus for fourteen hours from Cuauhtemoc to Zacatecas, approximately 650 miles (1,040 kilometers). This cut off at least three weeks of fierce headwinds.

Tarahumaran ladder descending into Copper Canyon.

Tim looking into an arid valley in the state of Chihuahua.

4 Colonial Cities and Cantinas

(June 1 –15, 2002)

Our bus arrived in Zacatecas right before sunrise. In the dim dawn light, we could clearly see a gigantic cross brightly lit on a high hill.

Zacatecas was once a wealthy Spanish colonial city, and the legacy of the riches dug from the earth are still visible in the elaborate architecture. We assembled our bikes and rode towards the city center (originally built for horses and carts pulled by burros), many of the roads were one way and so narrow that a modern car could barely fit. These historic colonial streets were made of cobblestones and tricky to ride because they were uneven, wet and slippery. We rattled past hundreds of years of history told in street names such as Plaza Independencia and Av. Hidalgo. We saw buildings with elaborate architecture carved in pink sandstone and an old aqueduct. We found the ornate main plaza and spent a few moments in silence sitting on an ancient wall while trying to absorb the scale and beauty of this fine colonial city.

I watched the bikes while Cindie searched for affordable lodging. While I waited, I watched an old man with two burros stop in front of a computer store to readjust the bundle tied on top of his burro. I can only imagine how much he has seen the city change in the decades he has been leading his animals through these winding streets.

Cindie returned with a key in her hand. Our limited budget reduced our lodging choices considerably. We pushed our bikes two blocks and carried eight panniers, tent, camp chairs and sleeping bags up several flights of stairs. The room had a bed that the two of us fit in snugly. We had barely enough room for our bikes and gear on the floor,

Cindie with a burro on the streets of Zacatecas.

Musicians in a restaurant.

and the room was poorly ventilated, but the location made enjoying the city easy.

After a rest from the long bus ride, we left our room to find the city awake and busy. Fruit vendors were common and Cindie had to try something from all of them. The fresh fruit available was papaya, mango, watermelon, cantaloupe, pineapple and jicama. She loves trying food that she has never eaten before. I decided to try cantaloupe; the locals put red chili powder and fresh lime on their fruit. It tasted like a pungent combination of sweet, sour and hot all at once. Cindie loved it, but I prefer plain fruit. We also tried roasted corn in a cup with cream, red chili, lime and goat cheese on top.

The following day we took an extended walking tour of the city; we spent half the day in the El Eden silver mine. The history of the mine was documented in the Pedro Coronel Museum, housed in the former Jesuit College. The Jesuits were kicked out of Mexico in 1767 by the Spanish crown, which felt threatened by the highly educated and compassionate priests. The Jesuits tried to help the plight of the indigenous people. The wealth from this mine may have glorified the Spanish empire, but it came at a terrible cost to the indigenous population in Mexico. They were enslaved and worked to death in this and other mines.

On our mine tour, we were lucky to meet a woman who was bilingual and translated the guide's talk. The mine had seen its share of history with tragic cave-ins and other disasters. Now, it's a major tourist attraction by day and high tech disco by night. It looked like an interesting place to have a drink. We walked back to our hotel room wondering what the indigenous miners would think of the underground disco today.

As we were leaving our room for dinner, we met Jose, the owner of the hotel and an avid racing cyclist. He showed us his collection of fine road bikes. Once a year he drove to El Paso, Texas to buy bikes, parts, and electronics. These imported items were much cheaper in the USA because of lower taxes. We made plans to go on a driving tour of the area the following day in his truck.

The next morning we met Jose and his wife, and they took us on a tour of the city and to the highest point in the area. Jose was excited to be our host and spoke in long complicated sentences that we couldn't understand. Cindie returned to our room to retrieve our Spanish/English dictionary because we had trouble communicating, Jose loved passing the dictionary back and forth looking up words. He wanted to explain many things to us and our dictionary made it possible. Like other Mexicans we had met, Jose didn't mind our lack of Spanish. He was delighted that we were trying to learn. Instead of becoming frustrated with us, he made a fun game of it. He told us that he was always treated well when he visits the USA and was happy for this opportunity to return the favor. We put many miles on our dictionary that day while our Spanish vocabulary was growing.

We drove for hours, stopping at various historical landmarks and received detailed explanations about each one. We eventually stopped at a little church in the middle of nowhere. This church was near the first mine in the area. Jose said that the conquistadors trotted down these same cobblestone roads on their horses. He truly loved the rich history of the city and the culture of his people. Jose made our visit to Zacatecas both memorable and enjoyable.

Leaving Zacatecas was hectic and confusing. The narrow city streets were crammed with cars, vendors with donkeys and pedestrians. Many people offered to help when they saw us stopped and looking at our map. After a couple hours, we turned off the main road and reentered the quieter and more relaxed farming areas. To our approval, the fierce headwind of northern Mexico didn't blow in this area. The

Colonial Cities and Cantinas

Cindie riding out of Zacatecas.

A street scene in Zacatecas.

bus trip had been a good idea. Our plan was to camp in the cornfields, but we found a cheap and inviting hotel instead. Cindie spent the evening writing her online journal and I experimented with writing short stories about our travels.

One Fine Day Down The Road

When we woke, we found cyclists occupied our hotel. Outside our door, we saw road bikes leaning against the wall and men walking around in spandex bike shorts. The cyclists ranged in age from teenage to retirement. After a short conversation in our limited Spanish, we learned they were a group of ten riders from Guanajuato who had stayed the night. They had their families with them. Mexicans rarely do anything unless they can bring their families along, and a week long bike tour is no exception. Unfortunately, they

Tim on a lonely road in the state of Zacatecas, Mexico.

Man plowing his fields the old-fashioned way.

were on their way to Zacatecas where we had come from. We would have ridden with them if they had been going our way.

For our next segment of the journey, we chose a route on the least used paved roads that we could find on our map. It was truly a zigzag path through the rural farm country of the Mexican state of Zacatecas. Except for generally heading south this road went no particular place. We were far from anywhere listed in our guidebooks. Based on the long stares and utter confusion on the faces of the local farmers there weren't many tourists about, much less foreigners.

We weren't the only people on bikes on this lonely road. Both automobiles and gasoline were more expensive in Mexico than in the USA. Most farm hands ride their old, one speed bicycles to work between the different fields. These bikes aren't found in the USA. They are heavy but reliable. We came upon several men wearing cowboy hats and jeans and riding between fields. Despite the lack of high tech equipment they rode well. I usually had short conversations with them involving how many kilometers it was before the next village and whether it was up or downhill. These tough, hard working men on bicycles earned our deepest respect. We were all cyclists, a common bond that transcends cultures.

We headed down the road towards Pinos, which was a dot on our map and several days away. We thought it might be big enough to have a hotel. We rode past a school where astonished children flocked to the fence and watched us as eagerly as we watched them. On the open road, we waved at men plowing fields with antique plows and burros. Time was standing still: men toiled in the same soil with the same farming techniques that their great grandfathers had used.

The nameless small villages along the way always had a plaza for resting and huge churches for exploring. We sat in the plaza, with no particular place to go and all day to get there, and gazed at the elegant church. It had so much detail in its facade we could have looked for hours noticing new things. It was obviously built on the great wealth of the local silver mine and on the countless broken backs of the enslaved miners. Suddenly, I noticed bullet marks blasted in the area around the bell tower. I showed Cindie, and we decided to examine them more closely. There were similar bullet marks around every window, but the bell tower had the most. After looking up a couple words in our Spanish/English dictionary, we asked locals about it. I didn't understand what was said back, but I did catch one repeated word. Revolution.

It's clear to me now. I envisioned a great battle. It was around 1810 or so and the revolution was sweeping through

Mexico. Now, if I were a Spaniard and an angry army of revolutionaries was coming my way I would head to the sturdiest structure around, the church. I would command my men to barricade the doors and take up firing positions in all the windows. I would send my best shots to the bell tower. The shot up condition of that bell tower today is testament of the fire fight that ensued to take this church. It's surprising that the holes were still visible.

We stopped in Noria de las Angeles to look at my crank because it had been making a clicking noise all day. This village had huge tailing piles surrounding it, which spoke of its history as an important mining center. Today, it's a sleepy small village where old women grow roses and men use pack animals to do their shopping. We even saw an old man come out of a cantina with a sombrero made of felt, not the tourist kind made of straw; it was well worn from many years of use. It was so big it easily could provide as much shade as an umbrella.

As we were resting, we saw fifteen packed buses turn towards the town plaza. The people on these buses probably quadrupled the population of this small village. Although it was early in the day and we had only ridden thirty-eight kilometers (twenty-four miles), we stopped to investigate. We came to Mexico to learn the language and culture not just pedal, and this looked like an educational opportunity. It turned out to be a political rally. People had bused in from distant rural areas to pump up the locals about a candidate. This isn't an every day occurrence in rural Mexico; farmers and their families came in from all over. Hundreds of people were milling around the square. We were easily noticed because we were the only foreigners around, and many had seen us earlier in the day riding down the road as they had worked their fields.

A flashy band played popular music, and many people knew every word of each song and sang along. In between

Band playing at the political rally.

These kids were interested in our map and bikes.

songs, a man was spewing out campaign promises. The locals looked as if they had heard these promises before and only wanted to listen to music. Eventually he introduced the candidate and his family. The crowd cheered and waved signs in the air as he shook hands and kissed babies.

As soon as we began trying to talk to people in Spanish about thirty kids mobbed us. They wanted to know all about our equipment and us. A few kids doing this were OK, but I was surrounded and started to wonder what would happen next. The flames of their curiosity were blazing and emotion was taking over: the kids had their hands all over our panniers.

They were squeezed in tight around us and there wasn't enough room for everyone. They began to push and shove each other to get a better look. In the middle of it all a women asked us if we needed any thing, and we said yes, anything to disperse the mob. Off to her house we went with at least twenty kids in tow; she was kind enough to let us use her bathroom. When we were done, we sat down next to a police officer and talked with the kids for a while. The kids calmed down in front of the police officer. I am sure he knew all their parents. I asked the police officer if there was a hotel in town. He said, no, but we could camp next to the police station. Once you have a Mexican police officer's permission to camp, his reputation rides on your safety.

We rode around town looking for a restaurant and couldn't find one, so we were once again back at the police station asking for information. They gave us directions to a restaurant, but we couldn't locate it.

We spoke with a group of women outside their house and asked about a restaurant. They said they could serve us food, but didn't have any chicken today. Chicken was eaten regularly in that part of Mexico, and almost everyone had a few running around his or her yard. We said we would be happy with eggs. She invited us into her house, and we ate at their kitchen table.

Three young boys lived in the house and they had many questions for us. We talked through dinner and beyond. We used this opportunity to learn more Spanish. We finally set up our tent just before sunset. Then the boys came over and asked us if we wanted to take a shower at their house. Of course we did. Meanwhile we met Victor, a local grade school teacher. After he heard us mispronounce many words, he decided that we needed to run through the Spanish alphabet. He obviously spent a good part of his day doing the same thing with five-year-olds in class. Each letter came with elaborate theatrics to help us remember the sound it makes. "Eh" is the sound that E makes, and I will never forget him hobbling around acting like a grandfather who couldn't understand me. "Eh - I cannot hear you." We could have stayed up all night talking, but I was exhausted, so off to sleep we went.

Days start early for farmers and their animals. We woke to the musical sounds of roosters, cows, horses, burros and all other forms of farm animals starting the day.

Now that it was light, it was more of a problem to use the bathroom. Cindie asked one of the friendly police officers about using their facilities and returned with a key to the municipal building.

After having coffee and observing the farmer's morning routine, we rode back to the highway to the village of Pinos. We joined several men riding to their fields and exhausted our Spanish vocabulary discussing how many kilometers it was to Pinos. They were startled when Cindie spoke, and they realized that she was a woman. We didn't see any women riding bicycles in the rural areas of Mexico. They were also learning something about a different culture. They tried to picture their wives riding with them and made many jokes. We understood little of the words, except the Spanish words for wife and bicycle, but men are men, and I caught the gist of it. By now, Cindie was used to this reaction; it had occurred every time we met men riding their bikes. She said, "Well at least they didn't try to race us like some of the other men did."

As soon as we pulled into the main plaza in Pinos, a little boy, about seven-years old, came running over to us and introduced himself as Francisco. He was excited to meet us and comfortable talking to us. Most children in Mexico were curious, but shy when they were around us. Francisco acted as if he greeted foreign cyclists in his village every day even though I am positive it's rare. I actually thought he was mistaking us for someone he knew well, his aunt and uncle perhaps. Francisco spoke quickly and endlessly about who knows what. Cindie was frantically flipping through the pages of our Spanish/English dictionary, but there was no keeping up with Francisco. He had a smile from ear to ear that spoke the clearest to us.

Moments later Francisco's mother arrived gasping for air and holding a steaming bag of tortillas in her hand. Her supercharged little boy must have run her ragged. We introduced ourselves and explained that we were looking for a hotel. When she heard me struggling with Spanish, she asked where we were from. When we told her "the United States," she told us that she had three brothers working in Atlanta, Georgia – the word "Georgia" was hard for her to pronounce. She turned to Francisco and tried to explain that we were from a different country, and we didn't speak Spanish. I don't think he understood this concept because he asked his mother if we were from Mexico City.

Francisco wanted to try on Cindie's helmet and sunglasses. She handed them to him and he put them on with a never-ending playful excitement. He wanted to come with us. He was so cute that I asked his mother if I could

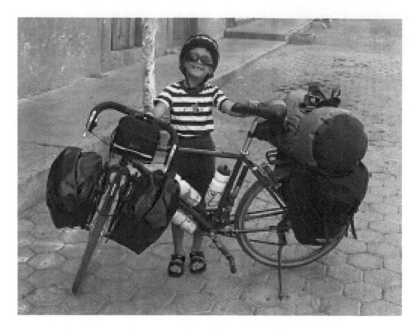

Francisco trying on Cindie's helmet and sunglasses.

take his picture. She fixed him up by combing his hair and straightening his clothes. He held his breath and waited for her to finish. It reminded me of the countless times my own mother did the same thing when I was a kid. I wondered if holding my breath would have made it any easier. Francisco grabbed Cindie's bike and posed as if he was the third member of our group. He wanted the complete look and wore Cindie's helmet and sunglasses for the picture. After taking the picture, I showed his mother on the digital camera's screen. She had a good laugh, and we showed it to Francisco. I offered to email it to her and family members, but I don't think she understood me. It was either my bad Spanish or the fact that internet or email hadn't yet arrived in this rural village.

We asked Francisco's mother again about lodging in town. She told us that there was a hotel and told Francisco to take us there. He grabbed for my hand but his hand was so little that all he could hold was one of my fingers. He took us to a hotel that we would have missed because there was no sign on the outside. We checked in and cleaned up.

Our room was better than our usual experience. It had a TV, and the World Cup soccer tournament was on every channel. Mexicans are passionate about their favorite past-time, and their national team was performing well. The game that was on didn't include the Mexican team so things on the street were business as usual. When Mexico is playing, the country is at a standstill.

That evening, I went down to the corner liquor store to buy beer. I walked in and found several old men in faded cowboy hats sitting around a rustic bar with shot glasses in their hands. The World Cup was playing on an old radio. To make conversation I asked when Mexico was playing next. They answered me harshly, but I couldn't understand them. Upon realizing that I was a foreigner, I think they forgave me for not memorizing the Mexican game schedule.

Their tone switched to friendly, and they began asking me questions. I had learned to recognize several familiar questions that inevitably were asked, including "Where are you from?" "Are you married?" "Do you have any children?"

When I told them that I was from the United States they became excited and asked if I had met their brothers or uncles in the USA. They pronounced their names slowly and repeatedly thinking that I surely knew Jose and Juan, but I wasn't understanding. These guys lived in a small town and didn't realize how big the cities can be or how far Chicago is from Arizona.

One of the men walked over to a large old oak barrel with a gravity tap at the bottom and a cork on top. He filled a shot glass and handed it to me. The room was silent, and all eyes were on me. I smelled it and said in Spanish, "Mescal, I like very much." They were surprised that I knew what it was and actually liked it. Mexicans consider mescal hallucinogenic, and only serious drinkers consume it. I believe it's hard liquor made from the agave plant, but then again, this Mescal didn't come from a bottle. This was homemade and obviously the village pride and joy. Mescal is quite good and to me tastes like thicker, more flavorful Tequila. I asked how much it cost, and they answered in long passionate speeches. One clever man held up some pesos in one hand, pointed at them with his other hand, and then pointed at me and shook his head "no," indicating that the drink was free. This doesn't happen every day.

This put me in a tight spot. Mexicans have an old and rich drinking culture. It's closer to a religion than a mere pastime. When a Mexican man offers another man a free drink, it's considered a great honor. It's absolutely unthinkable in a place like this to refuse a free drink. I also knew once the drinking started it would be hard to stop. The boys in the bar wanted to know how much the large foreigner could drink. As a traveler, I must accept cultural things that I do not fully understand, do things that I would not do in my own country and generally go with the flow. This is what traveling is all about, trying on someone else's culture.

There was no way I could ever keep up drinking with these guys. They practiced a lot and could drink the best under the table. I thought about my situation, but I really had only one choice. I poured the gold tinted liquor down my throat and tried not to flinch. It tasted good, and I expressed this on my face and said "Viva Mexico!" The boys all cheered and poured me another shot.

I tried to take my time with this one. The men introduced themselves one by one and politely shook my hand. A song came on the radio and all the guys stood in a line with their arms around each other and sang along. I think it was the Mexican National Anthem. My drink had to be finished before I was placed in the line with my arms around the guy next to me. They elbowed me until I sang along as well. Singing an unknown song in an unknown language was difficult. I tried to follow along with them but only produced a confused hum. This must have been good enough because another shot of Mescal was placed in my hand.

I had to find a way out before I finished this drink. I thought of what could pull even the hardest drinking man from the bar. I looked at my watch and said in terror "esposa" – wife in English – implying that Cindie was expecting me back home. They saw what was coming but tried to stop me anyway. They knew that if one of their wives wanted them home they would be marching off as well. I offered again to pay for my drinks. I think this was socially the wrong thing to do and even a little insulting because the men frowned, said nothing, and looked at the floor. However, they let it slide because it was obvious that I was unfamiliar with their customs. Every man in the bar had to say good-bye to me personally with long handshakes accompanied by parting words. I wish I had known what they were saying, but slurred Spanish was out of my league. I recognized the words "luck" and "god" so I guessed they wished me well on my journey. Of course, they wanted me to have one more shot for the road, and I couldn't say no. I threw it down my throat and slipped out the door. A man popped his head out of the bar and handed me the beer that I had bought when I first had walked in. These men were more than honest.

On the walk back to the room, I was feeling funny but not drunk. Cindie was concerned when I returned to the room. Apparently, I had been gone for quite a while. I told her about homemade mescal and the friendly boys at the bar. We drank the beer and watched soccer until we went to bed. In the middle of the night, I woke up with a painful nauseous feeling that sent me to the toilet. Cindie took my temperature and found that I had developed a fever. This always sends "mother hen" into a panic.

It turned out that Cindie wasn't overreacting. I was sick. There is no way of telling what caused it. Logic points to the homemade mescal, but it could have been anything that I had eaten. The problem with that theory is that Cindie and I eat almost exactly the same things. Logic usually wins these types of debates.

Whatever caused it I was sick for several days, and we stayed in Pinos longer than we expected. This turned out to be a good thing because Pinos was an interesting village with hidden colonial buildings and a rich history. When I was finally well enough to ride, it looked like rain so we stayed one more day. The weather turned out to be manageable, but I think we both enjoyed Pinos so much that we wanted to stay longer. We reluctantly left the next day. As we were leaving town the doors to the bar flew open and a group of men waving bottles in the air yelled "Adios, Timatao!" (Good-bye Tim)

It was only a few days ride to our first, planned long break of the trip in the popular colonial city of Guanajuato. A Spanish immersion school was waiting for us there. We were frustrated with our lack of Spanish and desperately desired to communicate on a higher level with the local people we met.

After leaving the Mexican state of Zacatecas, we entered the Mexican state of Guanajuato located in the heartland of Mexico. We made a stop in the important historical city of Dolores Hildalgo. This is one of the most important historical places in Mexico, and most Mexicans visit this city sometime in their lives: it's the birthplace of Mexico's independence from Spain.

Dolores Hildalgo was a Catholic priest who in 1810 stood on the now famous church steps and gave a pivotal

A very small hotel room.

speech known as the "Cry of Independence." This encouraged Mexican peasant farmers to lay down their plows and take up arms in a long and bloody war against Spain for independence. Unfortunately, not all brave farmers would return to their fields.

After visiting the historical sites, we checked into the smallest hotel room yet. Our two bikes, panniers and bed took up all the floor space; we barely had enough room to use our camp stove for coffee in the morning. As budget travelers, we have to be flexible and put up with anything for a night.

The next day we rode towards the city of Guanajuato. We had a steep climb with switchbacks but were rewarded with a picturesque campsite in the mountain pass. After a good night's sleep in the cool mountain air, we rapidly descended into the congested city of Guanajuato.

Cindie catching up with a cart pulled by a burro.

5 Overcoming the Language Barrier

(June 16 – July 17, 2002)

In the summer, parties and street carnivals spark life into Guanajuato almost every day.

When we rolled into Guanajuato, a fiesta and parade choked the streets with spectators and all manner of colorful floats and indigenous dancers. We followed the only moving lane of cars for a couple blocks thinking that we could bypass the confusion and reach the city center. To our horror, we saw the slow moving bumper-to-bumper cars being swallowed up by a narrow and completely dark tunnel. This dark narrow tunnel was a death trap for cyclists. We scrambled onto the sidewalk. The only above ground traffic to downtown was the endless stream of people in the parade.

Cindie took the lead and squeezed in behind a school group and, realizing her great idea, I quickly joined her. We slowly rode our bikes through the narrow crowded streets. No one was sure if we were part of the festivities or not. When the parade reached the main plaza, we exited and found a place to sit.

The main plaza must have been a magnet for English speaking tourists because several foreign tourists spoke with us. They told us where the cheaper hotels were located in Guanajuato. I watched the bikes while Cindie looked for rooms.

Guanajuato is expensive compared with the other places that we had visited in Mexico, and a cheap room was difficult to locate. We found a dark musty place that was almost in our budget and left the noisy street behind.

Cindie slipping in behind the parade in Guanajuato.

We immediately started intensive Spanish language classes. We stayed for four weeks and improved our knowledge and use of Spanish dramatically. I believe that it's a common misconception that being in Mexico or otherwise immersed in Spanish is all that you need to learn the language. This theory appears to be true for children who are developmentally learning language, but once you get to adulthood you have to work at it.

While we were attending Spanish school, I made up a flyer about our trip; it included a map of our world journey, photos and an explanation of our trip in English on one side and Spanish on the other. Torinston, a teacher at the school, assisted me with the translation into Spanish. We carried copies of this flyer in my handlebar bag and handed them out to anyone who asked us questions about our trip. At first, we encouraged people to read the flyer; by the time we reached Panama we could discuss our trip in Spanish.

Overcoming the Language Barrier

One of many colonial churches in Guanajuato.

Cindie and I felt we finally learned enough basics of Spanish to pick up the rest in conversation while on the road. I now generally understood people, and my vocabulary was finally large enough to convey basic ideas. Cindie worked harder at it and easily surpassed me. I planned to catch up while practicing on the road. In the small country villages we frequented, it's customary for the man to do most of the talking in restaurants, hotels and in all matters of money. Often Cindie would ask a man a question in Spanish, and they would turn to me to deliver their answer. Cindie found this annoying at first but eventually accepted it as something she couldn't change.

Besides learning Spanish several other things happened during our stay. I found the closest Internet Cafe to our hotel room and asked to see the owner. She went to work on my laptop and set my network parameters to work with her system. I was now connecting to the World Wide Web. I was excited and spent several hours posting pictures, sending and receiving email. The last time we had been able to send and receive email had been in Cuauhtemoc, a couple weeks earlier. That night in our hotel room, while Cindie studied Spanish, I answered email and placed it in the "out box." I sent it the next time I plugged in at the Internet Cafe.

At this point, I started looking at our Web site differently. At first, I saw it as a way to communicate with friends and family; however, now it was evolving into a way for us to document our trip. It was the perfect way to arrange and store all of our photographs and organize Cindie's daily journals. The number of visitors had picked up because several major search engines had found the site and slow trickles of visitors were signing up for my fledgling email newsletter. I had no clue how much our Web site was about to explode with visitors and change our lives in the near future. To me it was still only our photo album and journal.

On the down side, we became very sick in Guanajuato. We spent about half of our time running to the bathroom. Even with drinking only purified water and following all of the standard rules of selecting and eating food, we still became sick.

Not only did Cindie and I battle sickness, but our laptop caught a virus as well. The blame is mine. I hadn't downloaded the most current virus definitions for my anti-virus software and caught a computer virus when I opened an email attachment. The first thing the virus did was disable my antivirus software. I had to run around town looking for a new CD ROM. It took some doing, but I finally found a disk, loaded the new software and killed the virus. I spent several hours in a computer repair shop and learned most of the Spanish words concerning computers. I gained lifelong friends in that shop and often email with them in Spanish.

La Valenciana Church near Guanajuato.

View of Guanajuato from above.

On one particular day, Cindie and four of her friends from Spanish school decided to go shopping in San Miguel de Allende, a city eighty kilometers (fifty miles) to the southeast of Guanajuato. Cindie best describes the day with this entry from her daily journal:

San Miguel de Allende is a fine-looking colonial city with lots of shopping and is a mecca for retired Americans. I hadn't been in a car much in three months and was looking forward to the speed of getting somewhere faster than on a bicycle. Shari was the driver; she, her husband and two kids had driven down from Alabama. Lauren was five, and Areanna was seven. Shari had a Ph.D. in Epidemiology, the study of how diseases are spread. After an interesting discussion on how infections are passed from person to person via dirty hands, I now wash my hands constantly. Terry and Michelle, mother and daughter, from Santa Cruz, California also went on the trip; Terry, the mom, was a vegan (a person who eats plant products only), an incredible undertaking in Mexico, land of meat eaters. Michelle, her daughter, had recently graduated college with a biology degree and was thinking about going into criminology with the FBI. Helen, also along, was from London, England. She had a degree in Latin American Studies and worked with the homeless in London. She was traveling by herself through Mexico for three months.

While in San Miguel, we took in the sights and did some shopping. A big merchant market in San Miguel had everything, such as full-length mirrors in pressed tin (my favorite), jewelry, paintings, blankets and T-shirts. Everything was fun to look at, but of course none of it would fit on the bike, so I didn't buy anything. I did a lot of window shopping in Mexico. We also went into a store that made everything – sinks, to door handles – out of copper. San Miguel was a great place to buy copper accessories. Terry and Michelle were planning to stay the night and go on to Dolores Hidalgo by bus in the morning.

The rest of us left San Miguel about 5:30 p.m. and we drove back to Guanajuato through the city of Dolores Hidalgo and over the mountain. We took a break at a restaurant at the top of the mountain. When we set off again everyone was buckled in tight. I was looking forward to the drive back into town. Guanajuato has many underground tunnels that route traffic under the city, a place I wouldn't ride my bike, so this was an unexplored part of Guanajuato for me. Traffic was heavy when we arrived in town, so we were bumper to bumper in the tunnels. These tunnels were a maze under the city; at least each tunnel was clearly marked where it went. People even park their cars in the tunnels. We finally turned off on Alonso Street to go to the hotel where Shari and her children were staying. Out of the tunnel and onto the busy street we popped. We had climbed out of the tunnel and now were going down a hill.

As we rounded the corner, Shari said, "Oh my God, my brakes aren't working!"

She tried for the parking brake, but we still didn't slow down. I realized that we weren't going to stop until we hit something. I looked over at the kids, and Lauren was still sleeping next to me while Areanna was awake. I braced for the impact and leaned over to hold Lauren in her seat. I was afraid she would slip under the seat belt. Since I was in the back seat, visibility wasn't good.

First, we hit a truck in front of us and to my disbelief, bounced off to the right, jumped the curb and hit the wall. Shari said something about pedestrians, but we were still moving. Then we hit the truck in front of us again and came to a stop.

Silence, then Shari said, "Is everyone all right?"

I said, "Yes, and the kids were OK too" and then said, "Oh this is bad."

Shari said, "What?"

I said nothing and jumped out of the car. I thought that when someone was in a car accident in Mexico they immediately were thrown in jail. I had visions of Shari going to jail and the kids crying for their mommy. I ran over to some pedestrians who happened to speak English and Spanish and asked them if Shari was going to go to jail for causing a car accident. They said no.

The people in front of us came out of the truck and they appeared OK. The truck damage didn't look too bad; a broken light and twisted bumper but the van had more damage than I thought it would. The hood was dented up, and the grill was punctured. A cop showed up next. We had traffic backed up in the tunnel and beyond, I am sure. The pedestrian I talked to said that she would translate for us. My Spanish wasn't good enough for a situation like this. The cop was skeptical about the failed brakes until he tried to move the car. He had to use the parking brake as he drove the car away. Luckily, we were close to Shari's hotel. Shari and I walked to where they parked the car. When we arrived at the car, there were four police officers and a crowd of people.

First, an officer wanted Shari's insurance and license. Shari called her husband on her cell phone while the crowd became bigger. Then the police told her that her car would be impounded unless she worked out something with the driver of the truck she had hit. Therefore the choices were settling on the spot or getting the car impounded. It was an easy decision: pay the man. In the meantime, the proprietor of Shari's hotel showed up. He also spoke English and Spanish. Then another officer asked Shari for her license and insurance.

What a nightmare. It took an hour and a half to sort things out. In the end, Shari gave the man a thousand pesos

(US$100) for his twisted fender with the option of more if he showed a receipt for additional work. We thought we would never see him again. We all had a beer after everything was over.

It could have been a lot worse. We could have lost the brakes on the mountain. I went to sleep glad to have a bike to ride instead of a car to drive. The ordeal was over for me that day, but a bigger nightmare was to begin for Shari. She had many days of frustration and people's hands were outstretched all along the way. She contacted her insurance in Mexico, and at first they didn't want to step in because she had settled at the scene of the accident. However, they did help her in the end. Shari's advice for anyone in an accident in Mexico is to go through the same procedures you would in the US. Call your insurance company immediately.

Chili Negado, seasonal dish. A plobano chili stuffed with meat and potatoes covered with a cream sauce and pomegranate seeds.

Tim and Cindie in front of Casa Mexicana with Oscar the dog.

6 What's That in my Soup!

(July 18 – August 22, 2002)

Guanajuato was fun; we learned a lot of Spanish and enjoyed a needed rest. After a month there however, I was bit by the rambling bug again and felt we needed to get moving. I yearned for the excitement of seeing new places and meeting new people.

Cindie, on the other hand, was sad to leave the friends she had made behind in Guanajuato. It took her more time to get back into the groove of traveling again. A traveler learns never to look back but always look ahead.

As always, the first day back on the bike was troublesome. Terrible traffic in Guanajuato and a blowout that destroyed my rear tire started the day. We had to abandon

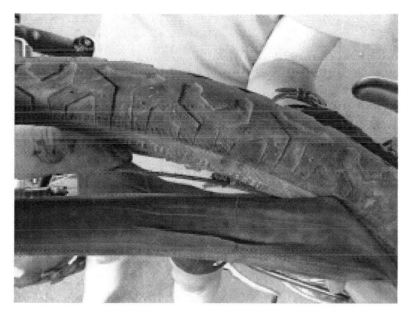

Tim's destroyed tire and tube.

the tire and resort to our narrow emergency tire that I carry for just such times.

The day became better. As we were limping into Irapuato, we met Rodrigo who was an avid cyclist. I knew he would know where the bike shops were in town by his shaved legs, Banesto racing jersey and the skilled way he rode his bike. Not only did he help us find a new tire, he also introduced us to his family who took us in for the night and fed us.

The following days went well. We left the big cities and busy roads behind and rode far back into the farmland and simpler ways of life. Several days of riding out of Irapuato, we found ourselves camping between the cornfields again. Michoacan has tall corn, proud hard working people, and endless kilometers of quiet roads. We entered a misty land of volcanoes and grazing wild burros. People here had time to stop and talk.

Cindie riding through a small village.

What's That in My Soup

Living in the shadows of ancient volcanoes has its advantages. The ash from previous volcanic eruptions fertilizes the soil, making it a good area to grow corn and beans. The people who work this land consider themselves lucky to live among such dark, rich and productive soil. When an old but wise man told me this fact during a rest stop, he whispered it so only the wind and I would know his great secret of a farmer's paradise.

We also noticed that fences in this area were made of large hard rocks that had flown from these volcanoes ages ago. These heavy rocks were basalt; the labor involved in clearing the land and building these fences was inspiring. One farmer explained to us the history of his land through the rock fences. "My father and I built the fences over there (pointing), and my father and my grandfather built those fences next to the pig pen, and my grandfather and his father built the fences next to the house, and.... When my son reaches twelve years of age, we will build new fences together in the cornfield to our south, and he and his sons will build more ...." I've never looked at these endless rock fences the same way again.

The days that followed were different then what we had previously experienced in northern Mexico. It was now the rainy season in central Mexico, and everything was green and damp. The scenery in northern Mexico had been dry and brown like southern Arizona. As we rode south, we gradually climbed to higher altitudes, and the landscape turned green, and the climate became humid. Instead of riding in the usual valleys lined by mountains we were now weaving around huge volcanoes and among ancient lava flows shrouded in mist. This produced a rugged and surreal landscape. Growing wild on the side of the road were bamboo, avocados and unknown plants with leaves as big as tabletops. Another surprise was the green carpet of moss growing everywhere. The rich smell of humidity lay heavy in the air.

Cindie waiting for traffic to clear.

During the rainy season from mid-July to early September, the rains began in the late afternoon. Being caught in a downpour made riding a bike dangerous, and we quickly learned to make camp before it started to rain. We camped in thunderstorms that lasted for hours and occasionally all night. A number of times after it rained, we crawled out of our tent to find ourselves camped on an island.

When we heard the first rumble in the sky, we knew it wouldn't be long before a thunderstorm was upon us. On this particular day, we found a grassy place between two cornfields and made camp. The sky grew black and the thunder and lightning moved towards us quickly. As it was starting to sprinkle, we threw all of our belongings into the tent and dove in for cover. We knew that the pounding rain would be arriving and we prepared to spend the evening in our tent cooking dinner and working on the computer.

What's That in My Soup

As the lightning grew frighteningly close – any lightning within five miles is frighteningly close for Cindie – we heard a truck stop directly in front of our tent. My heart rate rose, and my palms got sweaty when I heard two car doors open and slam shut, and then footsteps approached our tent. Cindie already frightened from the storm, was in a panic and practically pushed me out of the tent to investigate the intruders. My first thought was that we had made it this far in Mexico without any problems, but time had run out. This was going to be it.

To our surprise, instead of hearing the deep raspy voice of an armed robber we heard little children yelling hello outside our tent. I unzipped the door and stuck my head out to find a little boy and girl giggling at our confusion. I scanned back at the truck and saw their mother who looked gentle and concerned for our safety. The kids told us that a large storm was approaching, and we had to come home with them. Their mother was much shyer than the children were, but she showed her concern by pointing at the lightning. She said that we could load all of our gear and bikes into her truck and stay at their house.

By this time, Cindie had crawled out of the tent with our Spanish/English dictionary. She heard the whole story and was ready to pack and go. The storm was on us, and it began to rain. I had second thoughts. If we pulled everything out of the tent and put it in the back of the truck, it would be soaked before we made it to their house.

The rain was picking up its pace, and Mom and kids retreated to the truck. I was standing outside in a steady Michoacan downpour and talking through a rolled down window. I pulled together my best Spanish and explained that we were already set up and to move everything out of the tent would expose our gear to the rain. The kids were nearly in tears because they wanted to take us home. We were like a stray cat that they loved and wanted to keep.

The mother, a clever woman, quickly came up with a solution that made everyone happy. She invited us to lunch the next day in their home. The next day was Sunday, which is a special day for Mexican families. After morning Mass at their local historic church, they retreat to their homes for an afternoon of family activities and a special lunch. As an extra incentive, she told me that she would prepare a special dish in honor of our visit. The recipe for this dish was passed down, from mother to daughter for countless generations. The kids were wide eyed in anticipation of what their mother was hinting at cooking. When mom finally said the name of this special meal, "Menudo," the kids burst into cheers of excitement. I didn't ask her what Menudo was because it was common knowledge and highly revered in this culture. I asked Cindie, in English, "What is Menudo anyway?" Cindie explained to me, in English, that Menudo was a soup made primarily with cow tripe. This was going to be an interesting lunch.

We were honored that the mother would go to such extremes to entertain a couple of foreign cyclists who had difficulty with their language. I accepted her invitation and arranged to go to their house the next day. Then thunder and lightning became more violent, which ended our conversation. Her kids were obviously frightened, and I knew that the same would be true for Cindie.

I crawled back in the tent and explained our new plans to Cindie who was trembling, reminding me of the little kids in the truck. She was happy not to be sitting in the back of a truck with all this going on, but she preferred a house to our tent. The storm raged for hours, and she slept little between those two cornfields.

The next day the sun was shinning, and we rode the short distance to the family's house. At the house, the kids ran out to greet us. The father, whom I hadn't met before, came out and welcomed us into his home.

Setting up camp just before a rain storm.

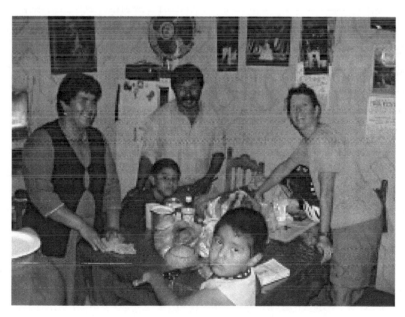

The family that invited us over for Sunday lunch.

It was obvious they had been cleaning the house in anticipation of receiving guests. I felt guilty for putting these generous people through so much trouble. The mother invited us to shower before lunch and brought us a bar of homemade lye soap and two clean towels. We were shown the shower, and Cindie went first. I sat on the couch with dad and our Spanish/English dictionary in hand. After wrestling with the TV antenna, he eventually pulled in a professional soccer game in the Mexican league. He tried to explain that this was either an old replayed game or that the best players are in Japan/Korea competing in the World Cup. I didn't understand half of what was being said to me. I was glad that we were watching soccer because at least I could understand what was going on even with the language barrier. Cindie emerged clean and fresh from the shower, and I took my turn.

When I returned from my shower, Cindie, Mom and daughter were going through a stack of embroidery projects. The father and his son were glued to the soccer game on TV and had saved the best seat for me. Rural Mexico is a traditional society where men and women's roles are clearly defined. I would pick soccer over needle craft any day. The mother left Cindie with her work and went in to finish lunch.

When we were called in, the table was already set with fresh cut flowers in the center. We all sat down, and Dad led us in grace while we all respectfully bowed our heads. As Mom was serving us, it was inescapable to ignore the little tubes that were ladled into our bowls. I try to have an open mind when confronted with the endless new things we encounter in foreign cultures, and I worked hard at it here. I was prepared to dive into this cultural treasure, but then an unwelcome memory from an anatomy class I endured in college popped unexpectedly in my head. I had a vision of dissecting a pickled cadaver's stomach. I clearly remembered the professor pulling out a handful of stomach, cutting it open and showing the class the different components that helped move food through the system. I had performed this procedure alone because my lab partner was queasy. I looked down into my bowl at the numerous cut up tubes and there it all was in my bowl. This vision was interrupted by a speech from Mom about how this is the exact same recipe passed down in her family and only made on special occasions because it takes hours to prepare. I knew that we were the guests of honor and the sole reason that she went to this much effort. To not eat and love every bite would be an unthinkable insult.

No one started eating, and it took me sometime to figure out why — except for Cindie who was turning white. She was obviously stalling wishing to avoid the inevitable. Everyone was waiting on me to take the first bite. It was a gesture of respect for the honored guest. I dug my spoon in and tried several times to keep the slippery tubes from sliding off my spoon. I smiled at everyone and shoved a spoonful in my mouth. The tension was broken and everyone started eating. It didn't taste so bad, but I couldn't get past the image of that cadaver in my mind and the feel of the stomach parts on my tongue.

Cindie didn't fair much better. She would pour her tubes into my bowl when no one was looking. This didn't work for long because every time her bowl was near empty, they filled it again. They thought that she loved it so much that she wanted extra. We eventually learned to leave soup in our bowls and act full. Sometimes travelers try food they like and sometimes they try food they don't like.

When everyone finished eating, the men retired to the family room to watch the remainder of the soccer game while Cindie stayed in the kitchen and learned more about traditional Mexican cooking.

By the time we said our good-byes to the family, it was late afternoon. As we rode down the road, all Cindie and I could talk about was Menudo. I said, "It did not taste bad, but I just can't get past what it is made with."

Cindie said, "I like the soup part," then sheepishly grinned and said, "Thanks for eating the tripe, I didn't want to swallow it."

We were anxious to return to our routine of riding until the rain started and camping in between the giant cornfields of the Mexican state of Michoacan.

We started out that day thinking that the next town was within two kilometers (1.2 miles). After we had ridden eight kilometers (five miles), we decided that maybe we went the wrong way. After another six kilometers (four miles), we stopped at a bus stop and asked a man where we were. We were off course. We decided to keep going and circle back at the next large town rather than turn around completely. We stopped in the town of Penjamillo. The town was too small to have a hotel, but a guy at the Pemex gas station took us to a place that rented rooms. We were right on the plaza. The room was huge; the ceiling was three meters (ten feet) high and had three beds in it.

We went scouting for a restaurant, and that is when we found the internet cafe. The internet had found its way to this small town in Mexico. We walked in and met Leslie who spoke fluent English, yet another surprise. It turned out that she was a teacher and was teaching class online through a school in Oregon. The curriculum was set up already; the teacher answers the students' questions via email and grades papers. Leslie got 240 emails that day. We arranged to meet Leslie and Bernardo, her husband, later on at the Internet Cafe. Bernardo took us over to meet his family on the farm. They had cows, pigs, goats and chickens, along with cats and dogs.

Later, we returned to our rented room. As we were settling in, I noticed some movement; it turned out to be a rat running around. After looking rat up in the Spanish/English dictionary, I ran out to the owner, told him there were rats in my room, and asked if he had a cat. He said, "No, but I have dogs." The dogs came into our room and chased the rats out; I made jokes about the great breed of Mexican rat hounds. We had a sleepless night. All I could hear was the scurry of rats on the floor. It made my skin crawl. In the morning, the owner seriously asked me if the rats had bitten us during the night. He was surprised when I told him no. We paid him the forty pesos ($4.20) for the room and left.

The next day we were riding into the city of Zacapu when we came across a little shack that claimed to have "Tourist Information." We stopped to ask about the location of a cheap hotel. Cindie woke up the man behind the desk. He said that he would have to call someone for help. When he stood up to reach the telephone, we saw that he was wearing a Mexican

Cindie with Bernardo's family.

97

police uniform. He firmly told us to "wait here." Our hearts stopped. We had heard from other tourists to stay away from Mexican police. They have a reputation for harassing and squeezing money out of foreign tourists. Cindie had said that the police at the car accident in Guanajuato were not very helpful. We waited in silence until a pickup truck arrived with several police officers wearing bulletproof vests and carrying pump shotguns. I reminded Cindie to keep smiling while I had visions of being in a dirty Mexican prison.

The officer in the shack spoke to the group of men in the back of the truck. We couldn't understand everything they were saying. I kept listening for the few words I knew describing hotels or lodging, but I didn't hear them. The entire group of men in the bed of the truck broke out into laughter, and I knew that our fate was sealed. They tried to ask us questions and explain something, but we were both trembling and preoccupied envisioning shallow unmarked graves. Our lack of understanding appeared to frustrate them.

The largest man of the group motioned us to follow the truck and we followed them down the street. I thought that they must have been taking us to their "special" place for foreign tourists. The flashing red lights and siren were on, and traffic cleared as we rode through town. The locals living in Zacapu certainly knew not to tangle with the police. We rode fast and furious to keep up with the truck that covered quite a distance in a short time because of the lack of traffic and of not stopping at lights.

To our relief we pulled over in front of a hotel and one of the police officers motioned for me to follow him into the office. The officer was gruff with the clerk and wrote a number on a piece of paper in Mexican pesos, which indicated how much we were to be charged for the night. I glanced at a sign on the wall that listed prices and noticed that we were paying about half the listed charge. The police officer noticed this, returned a big smile, and said, "Amigo."

I returned to Cindie and the truckload of armed police officers. I told Cindie about the great deal the local police department secured for us. Things were going so well, I asked if I could have my picture taken with them. They responded with big smiles and gathered around my bicycle for the photo. This event taught me that you couldn't believe everything you hear and shouldn't give in to stereotypes.

Tim and our Mexican police escorts.

We stayed one night in Zacapu. We continued to ride south towards Morelia and more remote areas of Mexico. To prepare for these long distances between cities we carried enough food for several days. When we left Zacapu, we were carrying one kilo (2.2 pounds) of coffee; a half kilo (1.1 pounds) of sugar; one kilo of oatmeal; a half kilo of raisins; bananas; oranges; a variety of soups, pastas and other dried goods. We bought fresh fruit and vegetables from people we met along the way.

From Zacapu we traveled to the city of Morelia. Morelia is an attractive city with colonial architecture. After a few days of rest, we continued east toward our next destination of Toluca, Mexico.

Into The Mist

When we arrived in Jose Morelos National Park the park attendants told us we could not camp there. We told them we were tired and could not go on. They looked around and then told us where we could set up our tent in the picnic area. We waited until late evening to set up the tent; by then most visitors had left the park. We spent the night without anyone asking us to leave the next day.

We spent the next morning drying the tent from the previous night's rain. The park employees stopped by to kill time and drink coffee with us. We had spoken with them for several hours on a wide variety of topics since arriving. Usually we only talk to people for an hour or less and the conversation is usually about the same introductory questions and nothing more. The park people cheerfully told us their views on politics, local road construction and the Mexican National Park system. If we didn't understand something, they would cheerfully rephrase it differently or give us the time to look words up in our Spanish/English dictionary. Two days earlier they had told us that we couldn't camp there and then decided to "let it slide" without any form of payment.

They were sincerely interested in us and we learned a great deal from them. We quickly became friends.

When we told them our plans of riding east, over the Mil Cumbres (a thousand hills) pass, they had a disturbing look of concern and fear. Their speaking quickened on this topic, and our understanding decreased, but we could make out something about remoteness and quick-changing weather. We generally got a warning from locals before setting out, and things had always turned out fine, so we paid little attention to them. We rode off as they were waving their hats in the air. They watched us ride out of the park and head east towards the pass. I believe they wanted to see if we were actually crazy enough to attempt the pass during the rainy season or if we were telling them a story to impress them. I actually saw both men cross themselves as we started up the hill. Little did we know that they were the last humans we would see until we crossed over to the other side of the mountain.

A twenty mile (thirty-two kilometers) climb took us up three thousand feet (915 meters). On climbs like this, we have learned to expect about four miles per hour (6.4 kilometers per hour) and many rest stops. I estimated the time to the top at about six hours and made sure that we had enough supplies in case something came up. The park employees all had agreed that water would be no problem and had told us of numerous creeks and waterfalls along the way. This was good to hear because water is heavy to carry. I only had packed enough for the day's ride and planned to filter the rest from a creek. I also saved weight on gasoline for the stove. We only had enough to cook one meal; I figured that we could build fires to make up the difference. This thinking was my first mistake. Making mistakes like this while bike touring in remote areas can cause a life-threatening situations – as I would soon find out.

The beginning of the climb was pleasant with the altitude keeping temperatures cool; the wind was nonexistent. We could see that the upper slopes were covered in dense clouds, which made for interesting scenery. We felt good, talked and joked for the first two hours. Time drifted by, and there couldn't have been two happier people.

After sixteen kilometers (ten miles), our ears had popped several times, and the drain of riding in thinner air started to creep in. We turned a corner and suddenly instead of looking at clouds, we were riding into them. I said symbolically, "Into the mist" to Cindie. Everything was damp and dripping wet. Visibility was down to a few feet and the road continued going up. The other funny thing was the absence of traffic on the road. We saw no one on horseback or lumbering along with burros. Not even the occasional bus. There wasn't anything but an eerie stillness. We nervously turned on our taillights and continued to climb.

The vegetation was changing as well. Instead of the bright green leafy plants and dazzling colorful flowers that we had seen on the lower slopes, we now saw dark green to almost black growth, and the air smelled of dampness and mildew. Everything was struggling to grow due to the lack of sunlight. The mist was growing denser with every pedal stroke and the silence was broken only by the "drip, drip, drip" sound of water oozing from thousands of soggy leaves and by our combined rhythms of deep heavy breathing. There was the occasional waterfall or rushing creek that we knew was there only from the roaring through the stillness. Visibility was too poor to see anything; even the lines on the road were difficult to locate.

At mile eighteen (kilometer twenty-nine) of this all-day climb, we broke free of the clouds and climbed above them like a jet airliner ascending to cruising altitude. The gray mist suspended below us looked unreal. When we reached the top, the temperature had fallen substantially. While we

Cindie is barely visible in the thick mist.

were climbing our bodies generated heat because of the large amount of work required to haul ourselves and our entire household up the grade; we were therefore still in bike shorts and short sleeve jerseys when we reached the top.

At the top, we were exhausted and started to think about camping. It was also about 3:00 p.m., and we knew that the afternoon rains could come at any time. I spotted a flat, hidden place to camp near the summit. It had plenty of firewood lying around, and I could hear a small creek rushing down the mountainside. We rode to the creek to make sure it was accessible and determined that it was hard to reach. Looking back, I think I was tired from going uphill all day and wasn't thinking clearly; I decided that a better place could be found further down the hill. This point marks my second and biggest mistake of the day. Given the time of day and numerous warnings from the park employees, we should have camped at the first good spot. Little did I know we wouldn't make it far down the mountain.

103

Every cyclist knows that descending is cold business. The wind washes away every bit of heat generated during the climb. We decided to pull on our jackets for the descent. Even though the weather was improving, Cindie put on her raincoat because of its wind-stopping abilities. I happen to find my fleece jacket before my raincoat so I put it on. It's warm, but not wind and waterproof like my raincoat. This was a lot quicker than rummaging through my bags again. I would later learn this would turn out to be bad luck or a bad mistake depending on how you look at it.

At first, the descent was everything that I had hoped. The weather was looking good. We passed a grassy area with a clear spring; it crossed my mind as another good place to camp. I was having too much fun to stop. We were weaving in and out of switchbacks but always going downhill. I noticed that we were descending back into the mist and thought that it would greatly slow our progress down the mountain. I also thought we would eventually descend below the mist. This was a fine thought but not reality.

Shortly after entering the mist, the sky opened up with hail. Millions of marble-sized ice balls fell from the sky without any warning. These frozen balls loudly hit the pavement and then bounced in every direction while others went rolling down the hill towards an unknown finish line. They were stinging my face and legs. In an instant, the road was obscured so completely that I couldn't tell the difference between pavement and dirt.

My first thought was that I must take care of Cindie. She has exceptional bike handling skills, but I wasn't sure she could handle riding on a sheet of frozen marbles. After I almost slipped and crashed, I decided that I wasn't sure if I could keep upright under these conditions. She was on her own. Every squeeze of the brakes produced a slide and slowing down took all my effort. My loaded bike suddenly felt cumbersome. I knew that this could be it. I kept listening for the terrible sound of my beloved wife crashing into the numerous things that could have killed her, but all I could hear was the pounding of ice, which was like a giant freight train running us down. A quick glance back revealed that she was controlling her machine like a pro and seemingly doing better than I was. This was good because running into me would have wrecked the both of us.

The best description of my attempt to stop was a controlled skid, and I use the word controlled optimistically. I knew I was still on the pavement because, besides the crushing of the ice, it was smooth. I saw a wide place covered in hail and hoped that it was a grassy shoulder. I headed for it in a do or die attempt to stop. The hail could have been covering rocks or mud, which would have definitely caused me to crash. I knew that continuing down this ice runway was going to spell disaster eventually. I could feel the point when the tires exited the pavement, and I pulled my weight far back; I knew that this was my best bet for survival if I hit a rock or hole. My fate was hanging by a thread, and I knew it.

As luck would have it, I found grass, and the one hundred pound bike I was attempting to stop was suddenly easier to control. I finally came to a stop and immediately looked back to see Cindie safely at a stop as well. My first thought was: what a relief no bloody crash to deal with in the middle of the Mexican wilderness. My second thought was: "What do we do now?" My third thought was: "BLANK!" I stood there panting and bewildered.

The hail was still pounding away, but it was starting to mix with rain. By now, we had spent enough time in this hailstorm for all the air vents in our helmets to fill with ice. When the rain arrived, it created ice water gushing down my face and neck. I suddenly felt cold, and I immediately became concerned about hypothermia. The warmest piece of clothing, my fleece jacket, was soaked to the core. The ground was ankle deep in water everywhere due to the sheeting effect of ice and rain falling so fast that it didn't have time to drain normally. My heart was still racing from a thousand near crashes I had just experienced trying to stop. Cindie was (uncharacteristically) calm and asked me what we should do next. She had to yell to be heard over the pounding of rain and hail. Seeing her look at me in that probing hopeful way cleared my head, and I started problem solving. I looked around and didn't see a sign of a house, barn or ranch. If I had, I would have been knocking on the door. No, we were on our own.

I tried to appear as calm as possible. Cindie was counting on me to get us through this situation. I had to act as if I knew what I was doing and had dealt with these adverse weather conditions many times before. The truth was I had never seen such a storm in all of my life. It had come from nowhere and caught me completely off guard. I had to regain my focus. I replied to her, "Get the tent up, get everything inside, and we will dry it with the stove."

Without questioning me (again uncharacteristically), she swung into action. She unpacked the tarp and covered my rear bags, the only bags that weren't waterproof, while I unrolled the tent. Once she finished she assisted me with pitching the tent. We calmly and efficiently put the poles together and put the tent up in our fastest time ever. This display of teamwork demonstrated how good we are together. This was no time to freak out. The rain was pouring through the mosquito net roof so fast; water was filling up the tent before we could get the watertight fly on. It was exposed to the elements for only a few seconds, but it took a real soaking. Cindie went into the tent to towel dry the floor while I finished staking down the fly. I pulled the bags off the bikes and handed them into the tent.

As I was handing her the bag with the computer (in a rubber dry bag) I saw that she wasn't towel drying the floor,

106

but instead had pulled apart our mess kit and was bailing water out with a pan like our boat was sinking. There were several inches of water in the tent. Despite all of the water falling from the sky, we didn't have any for drinking. I set our largest pan outside and watched it fill with water before my eyes in a couple minutes. At least that problem was solved.

I was still outside and starting to shiver. When Cindie finally told me that she was ready for me to come in the tent, I was losing motor control and had trouble getting my wet clothes off. I was extremely cold and stiff. We had several hours of climbing, the terrifying skating rink descent, and now I was soaked to the bone and fading fast.

Cindie had managed to remove most of the standing water. The rest had pooled in the downhill corner of the tent. The rain was still falling and flowing under the tent even though I had placed the tent on the highest ground around and on a noticeable slope. Rain was still sheeting across the ground everywhere. This made the rubber floor cold so we sat on our damp camping chairs. Our gear was perfectly dry thanks to the waterproof panniers, but the floor and walls of the inside of the tent were dripping wet. I was having trouble controlling my shivering and had a lot of difficulty lighting our stove.

My Boy Scout Master, Mr. Dawson, taught us boys that flames were strictly forbidden inside of tents because of the obvious fire danger. He often recounted several horror stories to us to reinforce this. He also taught us wilderness survival skills including the dangers of hypothermia. He had equally gruesome stories for this. I considered this information but continued lighting the stove. It was my best chance. I was in the initial stages of hypothermia and needed to warm up fast. I finally got the stove burning properly and the tent immediately began to warm up. My shivering subsided, and I regained enough motor control to change into dry clothes.

Of course, my warmest piece of clothing, my heavy fleece jacket, was rendered useless by being turned into a saturated sponge. If I had worn my raincoat like Cindie, I wouldn't be having these problems.

Things were improving. The stove was quickly drying everything inside the tent while the storm was starting to weaken outside. It was becoming dark, and the outside temperature was falling rapidly. The temperature inside the tent was climbing, and we were able to turn the stove down. Cindie started going through our food supplies and making a large pot of soup and pasta. Eating hot food was the ticket to my recovery, and soon I was feeling comfortable again. Now the problem was that I didn't have much fuel left and feared that the stove wouldn't last much longer. I shook the fuel bottle to feel the last precious drops of Mexican gasoline. I wished I had filled it before entering the wilderness instead of trying to save weight. All the mistakes I had made earlier had caught up with me.

The rain stopped, the ground drained, and I went outside to fetch more drinking water. I stumbled out of our warm tent and was greeted with clear skies. The moonlight was illuminating our surroundings and I could see the stars. Patches of snow (more like hail) had accumulated while we had been in the tent. I didn't think this was possible. We were in Mexico and at latitude well below that of Havana, Cuba. At least the river that once had covered the ground was gone and our ark of a tent was on solid ground.

I crawled back into the tent where Cindie had made our bed. As I warmed myself next to the stove, I couldn't believe that it was still running and wondered what it was using for fuel. Our cloth castle actually looked dry enough for sleeping thanks to the stove. At least one of my mistakes wasn't as big as I had thought. We turned off the stove and slept well. It had been an eventful day.

What's That in My Soup

In the morning, we woke to the strange sound of a car driving by us. It sounded like we were camped right next to the road. Upon closer inspection, I found the tent was a bike length from the edge of the road. The sun was out, and the patches of snow were melting quickly. We packed the tent wet and headed into the next town. It took us an hour to ride into Ciudad Hildalgo. We could have easily made it the day before if the hailstorm hadn't stopped us in our tracks. Again, we had adjusted to the changing situation, a normal occurrence while traveling by bicycle.

This experience in the sudden foul weather in the high Michoacan mountains was a challenge to overcome, but we had survived. A bad situation like this isn't without its benefits. I learned that when Cindie and I worked together as a team, we could overcome and accomplish anything. I truly believed that we would make it around the world.

After our ordeal in the high mountains of Michoacan, we spent almost a week in Ciudad Hidalgo. This town of ninety thousand people won't be found in any tourist guidebook or literature.

We checked into a hotel we found on the main road. The girl behind the desk told us that a woman riding a bicycle was also staying at the hotel. We left a flyer about our trip at the front desk and proceeded to carry all our gear up to our room. An hour later, Marta was knocking on our door. She was from the US and teaching English in Ciudad Hidalgo. She was our gateway to being invited to numerous social events and family gatherings.

Ciudad Hidalgo has a great market. It had specific sections for meat, vegetables, food stalls, housewares and clothing. Grocery shopping is a different task in Mexico than in the USA. People buy their meals daily and the produce and meat are fresh from the farm. We started buying our breakfast from the street stalls when we could.

Our emergency campsite the morning after the hailstorm.

One morning Cindie bought attole and tamales for break-fast. Attole is a type of cornmeal drink; the flavors available that morning were blackberry and chocolate. It also comes in rice flavor. The tamales, cornmeal paste wrapped in corn husk, were either dulce (sweet, a bright pink), verde (green and mildly hot), or spiced with chili peppers which was very hot. Cindie and I liked attole so much we would have it for breakfast when ever we could find it. We liked the taste of attole and the quick energy it provided.

On the final pass before Toluca, Mexico, the road climbed 915 meters (three thousand feet) in twenty-four kilometers (fifteen miles). Short but steep.

We enjoyed an uneventful climb until a pack of dogs attacked us. This attack was more vicious than most that we had experienced on the bike, probably because we were riding uphill and going slow. No less than five dogs came at us, and they had a violent distaste for foreign cyclists. The dogs split up; three came after me, and two went after Cindie. A great battle was waged. One of the dogs bit my rear pannier, and I had to drag him along for three feet (one meter) before he finally let go. The battle went on forever. We scarcely got away. I had to ram the leader with my bike before the pack would give up.

The closer we came to Toluca, the more traffic increased. On the ride through Toluca, to the city center, we battled buses and taxis for space on the road and oxygen in the air. Toluca is a prosperous and expensive city for Mexico, so finding a cheap room was difficult. We went to five hotels before we settled on the least expensive. Our hotel was a flashy place complete with a bellhop and elevator. We spent a week in Toluca visiting the velodrome, watching a bike race and going on a bike ride with the local club.

Women rolling tortillas.

Busy road on the way to Toluca.

7 Our Mexican Pilgrimage

(August 23 - October 11, 2002)

From Toluca, we went southeast to the picturesque town of Malinalco. This involved a steep but short climb out of the Toluca valley to our greatest elevation to date of 10,150 feet (3,096 meters). From the summit, we could see one mountain range after another. It was beautiful and frightening at the same time. The drop off was so big it was as if the earth was disappearing below us. On the way down, we had to stop and let our brakes cool several times. The vegetation changed from damp cool forests to humid tropical green bamboo and banana plants. When we finally reached Malinalco's cobblestone roads, I looked at my altimeter and was alarmed to see that we had descended five thousand feet (1525 meters) since the last time we pedaled. I also noticed that the air

Aztec ruins high above Malinalco.

Augustinian church in Malinalco.

was thick, heavy and much warmer than before. There were unknown flowers and plants everywhere.

Malinalco had narrow cobblestone streets and was surrounded by mountains. The town cannot be seen from above because it's hidden among dense green vegetation. We spent a day climbing up to the local Aztec ruins and exploring an ancient Augustinian church and monastery. We ate ice cream sold by an old woman pushing a vendor cart around the plaza. The day we left, we took a wrong turn and became lost riding out of town. We rode for thirty minutes before we found our way; we had our fill of riding loaded touring bikes on moss-covered cobblestones.

The ride to Chalma was too hot to be comfortable. Children played in dirty creeks while men slept in the shade. The dogs seldom woke up from their afternoon slumbers when we rode by. The road climbed gently from Malinalco until we reached the outskirts of Chalma. Then the road turned sharply up and we shifted to our lowest gears (22 x 34). Instead of spinning (turning the pedals quickly in a low gear), in this less than 1:1 gear, I found myself standing on the pedals and grinding until I reached the top. Cindie had to get off and push her bike up the hill. This road was so steep that people put rocks under their wheels when they park. Kids watching us ride up the hill from the back of their dad's pickup truck cheered us on.

At the turnoff to the famous church, we sat down at a makeshift restaurant to refuel. During lunch of some kind of soup and a large stack of tortillas, we agreed that this was the steepest grade that we had encountered to date – unless you count the elevator, we rode in Toluca.

We didn't know what to expect in Chalma, but our guidebook said it had one of Mexico's most important religious shrines. Allegedly, an image of Christ miraculously appeared in a nearby cave. This image was moved to the church and is highly regarded among Mexicans as a "must see" on the religious trail.

Chalma is a small village of about one thousand people. There were all manner of buses, taxis, horses, and burro trains arriving in town as we ate lunch. We also noticed hordes of people with backpacks and walking sticks marching into town; they looked sunburnt and tired as if they had

Pilgrims on their way to Chalma.

Tim standing next to a restaurant in Chalma.

walked a long way. Some of them were carrying large, heavy wooden boxes on their backs with statues of the Virgin Mary or Jesus enclosed in glass. Most people had elaborate crowns of flowers on their heads. We asked around and learned that the next day was the village of Chalma's annual birthday celebration. The people we saw were on a pilgrimage to this special place. We also learned that thousands more were on their way. All of them walked for days to show their devotion. The people that carry the heavy wooden shrines on their backs are doing this for their village churches. These portable shrines sit in their churches all year long except when carried to a religious festival. The porters of the shrines are heroes among the people in their village. It's a great honor to suffer in this way. Carrying this heavy weight looked difficult. We felt as if we fit in here. We must have looked as if we had come a long way on our bicycles to attend this special day.

Everyone was setting up camp and sanitary conditions were deteriorating. I noticed that many of the men were drinking heavily. Pilgrims who finally made it to town were ecstatic, and occasionally they cried and fell to their knees to pray. The whole scene looked like a combination of a tent revival, Boy Scout outing and drunken high school party. The church was too crowded to get close enough to see the famous image of Christ in stone. The streets were overflowing with pilgrims. How could more be on their way?

We had to be patient to get our bikes through the crowd and back on the open road toward Cuernavaca. By the look of the road out of Chalma, we knew that we had a long climb in front of us, but didn't know how big. At least the grade was gentle and we could comfortably spin the pedals in a low gear and talk. We were the only ones leaving town. We rode past an endless stream of staggering pilgrims going to the already overcrowded village of Chalma. They barely noticed us even though we were riding slowly up the hill. They were preoccupied with their mission.

After several hours of climbing, the temperature dropped and cycling was comfortable again. We came to a small village that had food stalls and pulque venders, which resupplied the masses walking down the road. Pulque is an alcoholic drink made from the sap of the agave plant. It's white, frothy and looks similar to milk. Pulque is considered highly nutritious even though it has the kick of a strong beer.

We asked for a place to camp and were told "anywhere" was fine. We got away from the mass of people and made camp. That evening I walked back into town and purchased a couple of liters of pulque for us to try. We sat and watched the sunset over the mountains while we listen to Radio Canada International on our shortwave radio and sipped pulque. It had a distinctively different taste, not bad, but I prefer a good Mexican beer.

The next morning we woke and did our usual routine of boiling water to make coffee and oatmeal. I lazily sat outside, drank my coffee and read a three-day-old newspaper while Cindie did her Yoga in the tent. As we were packing, we noticed that the road was filling with cyclists. One of the bikes was pulling a makeshift trailer with a ten-foot (three meters) high wooden cross erected on it. Most of the cyclists were teenage boys that were riding every kind of bicycle from heavy one-speed beasts to expensive sleek new road bikes. They were on their way to Chalma to join in the celebrations.

We left the mob behind and continued to climb. We had thought that we were near the top of the climb the night before. Instead, we continued to climb for another day.

We finally found the turn to Cuernavaca and asked people about the faint road on our map. Several people were completely unaware of a road going east to Cuernavaca (even though it was clearly signed); they only knew about the main busy road to the north. We asked two old men riding rickety bicycles about the condition and length of the road we planned to take. They had an animated disagreement over the numbers. The truth was elusive. My Spanish was improving, but I was still unable to catch the whole story. I believed one of them told me that it was all paved but four kilometers while the other insisted it was six. Neither had a clue as to how long it was. By the time I was done talking to them I wasn't sure that either of them had ever been out that direction before. I was only sure that the road was longer than I could see and ended before it hit the Gulf of Mexico. When I asked if they would like to join us riding to Cuernavaca they looked at me as if I was crazy. As we rode away, they both gave us big toothless grins and waved their hats in the air.

We were already over seven thousand feet (2,135 meters) and knew Cuernavaca was a little less than four thousand feet (1,220 meters). Somewhere there had to be a descent. We climbed another six kilometers (3.7 miles), and then the road turned to dirt. At first, we saw a road crew working on the road, then we saw a big sign next to the road announcing how soon the road will be paved all the way to Cuernavaca. The date on the faded sign was 1998; it was now 2002, and the road was still not paved. The dirt road slowed us down, but the absence of traffic and the quietness was worth the trade. We rode through a pass somewhere over 8,500 feet (2,593 meters) and dreamed of a long gradual descent. We descended about one thousand feet (305 meters) then climbed right back up to where we had started.

We did this a couple of times and finally came to a settlement with a one-room schoolhouse with a wood burning stove. We were ready to stop for the night and needed water for cooking and cleaning. I asked a group of surprised locals

The view out our front door.

if I could fill our ten-liter (2.6 gallon) water bags from the
faucet. They said yes, and then we pedaled off to camp on a
hill overlooking a green valley. That night we listened to FM
radio from Mexico City. I could pick up at least twenty-five
strong stations. The variety ranged from Mexican Ranchero
music to political discussions. We were so close to Mexico

City, a hundred kilometer (sixty-three miles), yet so far from anything. I slept well in the cool mountain air.

The next day we continued climbing and descending on the dirt road until we came to a high pass and could look down forever. This had to be the last hill; we had a long way to descend to the city in a short distance, and the road looked steep. By this time, we had ridden twenty-nine kilometers (eighteen miles) of dirt road over the past two days. Both the old men at the turnoff had been far off the mark. On the way down, we couldn't go much faster than on the way up because the road dropped quickly and was rocky. We passed several muddy men leading horses carrying firewood. They smiled and waved enthusiastically back at us.

When we reached the pavement, we were surrounded by luxury homes in an upscale neighborhood. We knew we were in the suburbs of Cuernavaca. Brand new Suburbans and Range Rovers replaced the occasional pack animal. What a contrast. We descended all the way into town, and before we knew it, we were both sitting on a bench in the plaza eating ice cream.

We stayed in Cuernavaca for several days. At this altitude of 5,058 feet (1,543 meters), it was over 95° Fahrenheit (35° Celsius) with 90% humidity. We broke a sweat just walking around town. Cuernavaca is a majestic colonial city with nice architecture and old Spanish built churches. We went to many great museums including Cortez's Palace. Because of the heat, we lounged around a lot.

We planned to meet a friend, Patti, from New Mexico in Mexico City in a few weeks, so we spent several hours on the Internet shopping; we had everything sent to her house to bring to us. In Mexico, biking and camping equipment costs more than in the USA; the difference is the high import tax.

121

Our arrival in Cuernavaca.

When we left town, the main road through Cuernavaca was closed because of a large street fair. Instead of looking for a way around, we rode through it. Because it was early, the vendors were still setting up their booths. The street narrowed, and we found ourselves riding in a tunnel created by tents of game booths and food stalls. The carnival went on for two kilometers. The Mexican people were polite and helped us move things out of the way when necessary.

We then rode past a huge Army base and had to pull over to check the map. The soldiers, standing at attention in the guardhouse, had a hard time not looking at us. I waved and one of them even nodded back. That day, we climbed over one thousand feet (305 meters) before we escaped the busy city of Cuernavaca.

After several moderate climbs up and down hills, we rolled into Tepotzlan. The tall mountains on three sides of town and the sheer cliffs create dramatic views. The town

Cindie pushing her bike through the street fair in Cuernavaca.

is a favorite relocating spot for Mexican artists and hippies. Long haired boys with guitar cases and barefoot girls with lots of beads were hanging out all over town. We found a room, cleaned up, and visited the church. We witnessed a small religious parade going to the ancient church that was complete with incense and fireworks. We stayed only one night in this strikingly beautiful place because hotel rooms were expensive.

The next day, as we were planning our route with the map, we noticed that there were two roads from Tepotzlan to Amecameca. The first was on the Autopista (freeway) and was the shortest. However, it was illegal to ride a bicycle on the Autopista. Only the rich can afford this expensive toll road. We read that it cost US$3 for every fifteen minutes of driving. The second was a country road and legal. However, it was ten times longer and descended one thousand feet (305 meters) into a valley. It would be necessary to ascend those one thousand feet again to reach the road to Amecameca. We chose the shorter route, the Autopista. We rode down the on-ramp and hoped that we wouldn't see a police officer. The police would surely squeeze a fat bribe out of us. After ten minutes, a Federal (Federali) police car zoomed by us, and I imagined that he flashed me an angry look, but he didn't stop. Luckily, it was a gradual downhill and we were off the Autopista in twenty minutes. At the tollbooth, a police officer with an M-16 assault rifle shook his index finger up and down at us, glanced around and motioned us through. Wow, we passed on through without paying a bribe or even being questioned.

Now we were on a quiet country road without traffic and started to climb once again. I looked at my altimeter and was shocked to see that we were at an elevation of 3,500 feet (1,068 meters). We hadn't seen an elevation this low since Green Valley, Arizona. This meant that we had a five thousand foot (1,525 meter) climb to reach Amecameca.

This climb took two nights and three days to reach the top. The riding was hot, over 90° Fahrenheit (32° Celsius) at first, but cooled off as we climbed higher. The first night we found a campsite in a farmer's field. It had views into the valley we had left and of the mountains that we still had to climb in the coming days.

The second day we had to leave our quiet rural road behind and join the much busier road to Amecameca. The traffic on this road was tolerable because the road was wider than usual. This road is the main evacuation route when the large active volcano Popocatepetl (Popo) erupts. For several days, we had seen warning signs on the road announcing that we were in an active volcano zone. The last eruption had been only two years before. Every business in the area has informational posters on how to evacuate when Popo blows his top. Everyone was nervous when we asked about Popo.

The second night of the climb we had a hard time finding a place to camp. We were tired from ascending the previous two days. After I filled our ten-liter water bag (2.6 gallon) at a store, I found a fruit orchard down a narrow rocky road that was hidden. By now we had camped all over Mexico, and nobody had kicked us out or bothered us. We pitched our tent among trees containing avocados, lemons, limes and many other types of fruits. After we had set the tent up and started dinner, we saw two boys walking down the road in their school uniforms. They were obviously going home. A few minutes later, a man came walking up the road to talk to us. He introduced himself as Pancho. I was ready for our first speech about private property before being kicked out. We were both too tired for that, and it was almost dark.

Instead, he invited us to stay in his house. He said that his brother's family was away in Mexico City, and we could stay in their house. He announced that his wife would make us dinner. I put my pan of half-eaten macaroni and cheese down and started to pack.

As we were pushing our bikes to the house, he explained the orchard to us. When we told him that we had never seen a particular type of fruit (I can't remember the name), he gave us some to take with us. He then borrowed my knife and cut one open for us to sample while explaining the whole cultivation process. The fruit was green on the outside; the inside was a white flesh with large black almond-shaped seeds. We carried the fruit for three days and then cut it open. Cindie said that we needed to wait longer for it to ripen. It had the texture of a pineapple and an unfamiliar taste.

Next, we met his wife Beatrice. They showed us where we could stay. We couldn't believe it. We had an entire traditional Mexican house to ourselves. They told us to roll our dirty bikes into the living room. That evening, after a delicious dinner of Chili Rellenos, Beatrice told us when the two boys had come home from school they said, "Mama, there are gringos in the orchard! Can we ask them in?" The kids showed us their favorite toys and books. I even helped the oldest boy with his English homework. I am always amazed at how much homework Mexican kids have. We saw them carrying books and studying in public places, regularly.

We slept well, and the next morning Beatrice had breakfast waiting for us. We ate, drank coffee and talked about the dangers of the volcano erupting and the problems of the USA and Mexico border. Mexican TV and newspapers routinely publish reports about fatalities of Mexican citizens that occur at the border.

Tim with Pacho, Beatrice and one of their sons.

We took pictures with the family and packed. They wanted us to stay, but we didn't want to strain their limited resources any further. The kids ran down the road with us as we rode away.

We rode another ten kilometers (six miles) up the mountain and found ourselves on flat terrain the rest of the way to Amecameca. We arrived in Amecameca at 1 p.m. and had plenty of time to sit around the plaza before getting a room.

The scenery from the town of Amecameca is stunning. Nearby, two volcanoes over 18,000 feet (5,490 meters) high tower above the city. One of them, Popo at 17,883 feet (5,454 meters), is the most active and has a permanent plume of smoke rolling out of its crater. The other, Iztacihuatl 17,318 feet (5,282 meters), is inactive and is permanently covered in snow. I have never seen anything like this before. Every day of their lives, the local people nervously watch Popo's smoke plume for any sign of changes. Here, the forces of nature rule.

From Amecameca we found several scenic day rides on quiet country roads. We explored numerous hiking trails around the base of the volcanoes. We liked it here so much that we stayed a couple of weeks and explored the surrounding countryside with its old Spanish missions and lazy back roads.

Our Bike-less Journey to Mexico City

While staying in Amecameca we became friends with the family who owned and ran the hotel. We asked them several questions about visiting nearby Mexico City. They warned us that riding a bicycle into the city was extremely dangerous. Amecameca is an hour away from Mexico City by bus. They told us we could store our bikes in an extra room for as long as we wanted. I trusted my instincts about the family and felt comfortable storing our gear with them. Without

Bike taxis in Amecameca.

the need for camping equipment and bike accessories, we could travel light. We scaled down to two small backpacks. Being separated from my bike felt like losing a limb.

Taking the bus to Mexico City was a completely different experience for us. We were accustomed to independently riding our bicycles and camping where we wanted. Now there were bus schedules and high-rise hotels. We were no longer a novelty of interest to locals. No farmers to drop their plows, sit in the shade and talk to us. We were suddenly every day tourists.

As unappealing as that may sound, we needed a physical break from the bike. Besides, the only agreeable way to see the marvels of Mexico's capital is on foot. During the bus ride into Mexico City, we saw crowded highways that would have been dangerous on a bicycle. Twenty-two million people live in Mexico City. Everywhere Mexicans drove in unfamiliar ways to us; here they added the aggressiveness of a big city. The thick foul tasting pollution that hangs over the city reduced visibility and made breathing painful.

One of the most memorable and disturbing sights was the endless poverty-stricken shantytowns that ring the city. It reminded me of pictures I have seen on TV of war

Beautiful, crowded and polluted Mexico City.

129

refugee camps. People on the bus told us the names of the more famous unofficial cities of poverty. We were told that no official numbers are kept, but the estimates run in the hundreds of thousands. Conditions were desperate, and I was glad to be on the bus. We found a hotel in the historic center, met our friend Patti from New Mexico and stayed for almost two weeks.

Our room was a few blocks from the Central plaza, El Zocalo. This is Mexico's heart and soul. We spent several hours exploring the Aztec ruins of the Temple Mayor. These ruins are adjacent to El Zocalo and the stunning Catholic cathedral. The conquistadors dismantled one civilization to build another.

Cindie and Patti's favorite site was easily the famous Aztec ruins of Teotihuacan. Here we could walk through palaces reserved for kings. The climbs up the Temple of the Moon and Sun, the third largest pyramid in the world, were tiring because of the many large steps. From the top, we could see for miles.

We all enjoyed the ancient Aztec waterway of Xochimilco. During the time of the Aztec, the entire Mexico City area was a lake with an elaborate canal system. Over time the city of twenty-two million had consumed the water from the lake and built houses where the canals use to be. Xochimilco, what is left of that ancient canal system, is a favored relaxing spot for the citizens of Mexico City. We hired a boat with a guide to propel us through the water. To add to the party atmosphere, Mariachi bands floated along in their own boats. They tied up alongside our boat and played a few songs for pesos. Old women in rowboats sold cold beer and snacks to tourists.

The Olympic Velodrome was my favorite place to visit. This was the place where Eddie Merckx made cycling history with the hour record. We toured the velodrome and watched training races.

Temple of the Sun, Teotihuacan.

Temple of the Moon, Teotihuacan.

The National Museum of Anthropology and Mexico City Zoo were both visited in a long day outing. Visiting them required a long subway ride across town, but they were walking distance from each other. The museum is world famous for its extensive collections of indigenous cultural artifacts. This included both past and present indigenous groups in Mexico. We recognized groups that we had already met while riding our bikes. I spent the majority of my time studying the indigenous groups of southern Mexico. We would be riding through this area in the coming weeks. This information convinced us to go to the Mayan ruins of Palenque while we were in southern Mexico.

The Mexico City Zoo is also world class. It is modern with spacious areas for the residents. It had large number of famous animals, including the Giant Panda Bears. The zoo was free admission as well.

The downsides of Mexico City included the construction that was going on around the Zocalo; it kept us up all night. Also as the days went by, we noticed the pollution in the air grew thicker. In addition, almost every time we rode the Metro (subway), we had thieves' hands probing our empty pockets. I felt violated when I found someone's hands in my pocket. Our guidebook warned us about pickpockets on the subway, so our pockets were always empty. Instead, to carry our valuables we use a money belt that is worn under our clothes.

Mexico City left its mark on us. While there, I had a sore throat that we didn't take seriously. It turned into strep throat or something similar. Cindie caught it from me and our friend, Patti, was also sick. It was exciting to visit Mexico City, but I could never live there.

Return to Amecameca

Returning to Amecameca was a big relief because it was smaller and less congested than Mexico City. We returned

The crowded Mexico City subway.

to our hotel, picked up our bikes and gear from the family, and moved into another room.

We remained in Amecameca for two weeks while we were sick. Cindie went to the pharmacist with our symptoms and he sold her an antibiotic. Prescriptions aren't necessary to buy antibiotics in Mexico. The same drug would have required a doctor's visit, a prescription and several times the cost in the USA.

We lay in our bed for days, postponing our departure from Amecameca waiting to get well enough to move on. We lost our fitness and got behind schedule. This isn't to say that we have much of a schedule. I like to say, "Our goal is to have no goal", but our six-month Mexican tourist visa was running out, and a loose schedule was necessary to avoid being an illegal alien forced to pay fines.

We had a month left on our Tourist Visa. After looking at a map and calendar for days, we determined that a bus ride was necessary to take us closer to the border. Being near Mexico City meant that there were nonstop buses departing daily for all points in Mexico. Bicycles are common on the bus and not a problem to transport.

The next decision was where to ride the bus. There are at least three approaches to Guatemala. The catch was that we needed to straighten out some banking business. We had to wait for paperwork to be done and find a city where Federal Express could send a package. This required a city with an international shipping office. This city also had to be close enough to the Guatemalan border so we could cross before our time expired. We were sad because we had planned beach time in Oaxaca, but there were no shipping offices in that direction. I was surprised how few cities in southern Mexico had what we needed.

We had a few choices, but Cindie decided that she wanted to see the famous Mayan ruins of Palenque. The city of Villahermosa was a few days bike ride from the ruins and had an international shipping office. We decided to take an overnight bus to Villahermosa and the low tropical plains in the state of Tabasco, Mexico.

Tim riding towards Amecameca.

8 Nightmare in the Jungle

(October 12 - November 7, 2002)

We stepped out of our air-conditioned bus at 4 a.m. and immediately began sweating in the tropical heat and humidity. We didn't know it at the time, but we wouldn't stop sweating and suffering from unbearable heat and humidity for the next three weeks.

Even though our guidebook had negative comments about Villahermosa, I found it to be a well-kept and prosperous city with friendly people and few tourists. This was a reoccurring theme. I must be an odd traveler. I like the "real Mexico" and not the made-for-tourists Mexico where the guidebooks herd the masses.

Villahermosa is the capital of the small but oil-rich state of Tabasco. Optimism and prosperity were evident everywhere; people had new cars, wore nice clothes and carried cell phones. This explains why it had an international shipper while much bigger cities didn't. It was also one of the most expensive places that we visited in Mexico. A hotel room with air-conditioning, something we couldn't live without, cost US $25 per night.

We completed our business and saw the sights, including viewing the ancient Olmec heads located at Parque Museo de La Venta. These heads are carved in hard volcanic rock (basalt) and are over ten feet (three meters) high. It is believed that the heads were carved sometime between 1150-150 B.C. The heads may represent warriors.

The day we left Villahermosa ended six weeks without exercise, and we felt this on the bikes. It was as if we were starting over again. My rear end was the first thing to remind me that I hadn't been riding. The heat and humidity were the worst. Even though we left at sunrise, 7 a.m., it was 90°

Tim standing next to an Olmec head.

Fahrenheit (32° Celsius) and 90% humidity by 9 a.m.

When we left town we immediately noticed that the landscape had changed from the high cool mountains of central Mexico. The state of Tabasco is covered in steamy lowland swamps and the exotic wildlife that lives in this habitat. Colorful birds waded through the shallow water and sang songs. Cindie pointed out a large iguana on the side of the road; I have seen smaller dogs. Tabasco's swamps are a perfect breeding ground for mosquitoes and all other forms of bug life. Anything that eats insects would have had an easy life here. Anything that is eaten by insects (us) had a difficult time here. This explained both why we saw such big lizards and why we used so much bug repellent. We also started taking Chloroquine, a common anti-malaria drug sold over the counter in Mexico, that tastes like a rusted car fender.

Nightmare in the Jungle

The heat was affecting Cindie. By midday, she was red in the face, had clammy skin and complained of a headache. I was concerned that she was suffering from a heat illness. I saw a hotel, and it was time to get her in a cold shower. We checked in, took a shower, and slept for hours under a strong fan.

The next day we set off at sunrise again and rode as much as we could before 9 a.m. when the discomfort of the heat became intense. To make things worse, a strong headwind had kicked up. Even though Cindie was taking advantage of my draft by riding directly behind me, she was starting to overheat again. This time there was no hotel for refuge. We would have happily stopped at any hotel for the night and even paid a kings ransom for one with air conditioning, but there were none. The only thing we could do was keep moving. We would ride for an hour and rest at various snack stores and truck stops for an hour.

I love Mexican truckers. They were friendly and always showed us great respect on the road. They knew the good places to eat. A half dozen tractor trailers pulled over at a restaurant was a good sign.

I finally asked one of the friendly truckers who knew the area about the location of a hotel. I asked (in Spanish) "Sir, how many kilometers is it to reach the next hotel?" He took a long breath and looked at Cindie, then at our loaded touring bicycles and then at me. Next, a big smile grew slowly across his face. He started asking all the usual questions with joy and enthusiasm. Where are you from? Where did you start today? Where are you going? Why did you choose to travel in Mexico? Do you like Mexico? Which parts do you like the best? …. To make a long story short I gave him one of our printed flyers with both English and Spanish. When I gave it to him, he looked at the pictures and put it in his pocket. I could tell by his reaction that he probably didn't read much and possibly not at all. This is common in this part of the world. I knew that he would have someone read it to him later. I acted as though I didn't notice, answered him in my best Spanish, and in the most respectful tone. After he couldn't think of any more questions for me, I politely asked him about the location of the next hotel again. He didn't hesitate in his answer: "After this place there isn't anything for the next fifty kilometers (thirty-one miles) until you reach the town of Palenque."

We didn't want to ride that far. It was one p.m. in the afternoon, 95° Fahrenheit (35° Celsius), and 90% humidity. A strong headwind felt like the hot moist steam that whistles out of a teakettle. My wife was in danger of seriously overheating, and my butt hurt. However, we had no choice but to push on. I reminded Cindie of the time we had been caught in a freezing hailstorm in the high mountains of Michoacan only a few months before. She wasn't amused.

When we finally reached the city of Palenque, we were exhausted. I was tired from riding into a headwind that slowed us down, and Cindie was tired from being miserably hot all day. I told Cindie, "We can stay anywhere you want as long as I don't have to carry these bikes up any stairs." Cindie was sensible, looked around, and checked prices at a few places. Air- conditioning was way out of our budget, but she did find a room that we could afford that didn't require stairs. We took showers, ate, and slept for hours.

Paradise Found

The next day we packed and bought groceries and gasoline for the stove. Our plan was to ride the eight kilometers (five miles) to a campground near the famous Mayan Ruins of Palenque and stay until we grew tired of it. This has become our regular habit: don't go to the next place until tired of the current place. This way we never felt as if we missed something or rushed through.

Nightmare in the Jungle

The Maya Bell campground was cheap, exotic and a paradise with monkeys, palm trees, thatched huts and thick jungle vegetation. This was an international travelers gathering place. We felt as if we were at a tropical beach with lazy days and little grass shacks. In fact, we had everything the beach has except the high prices and an ocean.

Camping in the jungle has its drawbacks. Our first night, we were introduced to the Howler Monkey. This small monkey makes a loud and ferocious sound. We thought gorillas were attacking our tent. Pesky ants quickly cover any type of food that is placed anywhere but inside the tent. The darn things bite.

In this humid environment, we always woke up with our clothes soaked from sweat. We tied our wet clothes on the back of our bikes to dry as we rode. Waterproof panniers do great for keeping the rain out, but they also don't

Our campsite at the Maya Bell.

let anything dry. Wet clothes get stinky fast when stored in our panniers.

We went to the nearby ruins of Palenque three times during our one week stay. The ruins are located on the edge of the Yucatan plateau (a limestone shelf) with sweeping vistas and giant jungle plants everywhere. I like ancient ruins enough, but Cindie absolutely loves them and studies every aspect of each site. I had to admit that the ruins of Palenque had been my favorite so far. It's a remnant of an ancient culture. Mexican and international archeologists have reconstructed many of the temples. We couldn't visit the famous Temple of Inscriptions because it was under construction. For hours, I sat in a privileged kings' temple and soaked in the place, imaging how things were back then, while Cindie ran around studying, deciphering and comparing the stone-engraved hieroglyphics. After hours of hiking from temple to temple, we decided to get something to eat out at the main entrance.

Tired and hungry, we were ready to return to the Maya Bell campground. Cindie was sad; I knew she would miss this place. Cindie was walking down a set of stairs near the Temple of Inscriptions and her foot came down on top of a rock at an awkward angle. Her ankle gave way, and I actually heard her tendon rip. Cindie said, "Was that my ankle I heard rip?" I looked down at her ankle; it had swelled up to a big knot in a matter of minutes. We limped our way over to the food stands, and I got her a big piece of ice to reduce the swelling. I told her to ice it, elevate it, and compress it. By this time the pain had kicked in, her adrenaline was up, and her blood sugar was down. Tears were streaming out of her eyes uncontrollably. Cindie sat with ice on her ankle until the chunk of ice melted. The woman who gave me the ice came over and tenderly examined Cindie's ankle. She acted as if she had done this before. Then she gave Cindie

View of the Palace, Palenque.

Temple of Inscriptions, Palenque.

a couple of bananas so she would feel better. What a nice gesture.

We stayed in Palenque an extra day so Cindie's ankle could recover before we started riding again. For the next six months Cindie was very careful not re-injure her ankle when she walked on uneven surfaces. She preferred riding because her feet were held in place by clipless pedals and reduced the chance for re-injury. Clipless pedals are a system like a ski binding that securely attaches a bike shoe to the pedal and holds the foot firmly in place; they are used for better pedaling efficiency.

Along The Gringo Trail

The road from Palenque to San Cristobal de La Casas is world famous. This stretch has excellent things to see including three unique swimming holes in rivers of deep blue water, two impressive waterfalls, the Mayan ruins of Palenque and Tonina and the colonial city of San Cristobal; all are located in the state of Chiapas, Mexico.

These attractions were the reason that we had come this way, along with tourists from all over the world arriving by backpack on public buses and on package tours in private buses. Called the Gringo Trail, this route is apparently considered dangerous by package tour groups. When they passed us on the road, their faces were pressed against the window with expressions of horror. During two of our rest stops, people actually took our pictures through the bus window.

Our first day out of Palenque was over 90° Fahrenheit (32° Celsius) and 95% humidity because we were still less than three hundred feet (92 meters) above sea level. We knew that in a few days we would climb to over six thousand feet (1,830 meters) and to cooler temperatures.

It was a short cycling day, three hours of riding, from Palenque to the delightful waterfall of Misol-Ha. Here the water drops 120 feet (37 meters) into a deep circular pool that is perfect for swimming. We walked on a trail that goes directly under the falls. Tour groups arrived in buses, stayed for thirty minutes, frantically took pictures, loaded back on their buses and left. After the last tour group left, we set up camp near the falls. The thundering sound of the falls soothed us to sleep.

Over the last few months of bike touring in Mexico, we had learned not to ride on Sunday. This is when the roads can have drunk drivers. We thought we could avoid the majority of problems by finishing early. However, Sunday on the Gringo Trail brought a new problem. On this hilly road from Mi sol-IIa to Aqua Azul, locals stop tourist vans and buses by holding a rope across the road. They then would ask/demand them to pay a toll. This is illegal.

I had dealt with this before on a previous solo trip in the area and learned not to panic or stop. Cindie and I discussed ahead of time what we would do in this situation. As soon I saw the rope across the road, I would increase my speed and Cindie would stay behind me as close as she could. The toll collectors would be faced with the choice of either dropping the rope to let us through or receiving serious rope burns as we charged through.

Even though I had experienced this before and Cindie and I had discussed this possibility I was still nervous. I wondered if they would physically hurt the both of us or if they were determined enough to knock me off my bike with the rope. The rope holders looked confused when we sped up towards them. The rope began to sag. It was like playing the childhood game of chicken to see who would bail out first. I had no plans of stopping. Fortunately, they dropped the rope. Still it left our hearts racing.

After a long unnerving day of Sunday craziness, we arrived at Agua Azul. Instead of a single stream of water falling from a great height, these falls are wide with a big sheet of water tumbling over several levels of rocks. We stayed for two nights and spent an entire day resting and swimming.

The falls at Agua Azul attract a large number of international tourists. Too many tourists in one area create a problem. It changes the behavior of the locals. I am always happy to see locals prosper from tourism. The problem is when the locals start thinking of me as an industry and not as a person. This greatly reduces the amount of meaningful interaction and learning from each other. The locals in these places only wanted to sell me something.

In Agua Azul, the level of petty crime was high. Several people working there warned us that theft was a problem. Therefore, one of us was with our belongings at all times. Cindie remained in the tent while I went swimming. When I returned, Cindie told me that a man silently walked to the tent, looked inside, saw her and ran off.

The falls at Agua Azul.

Nightmare in the Jungle

The next day we climbed out of the hot steamy jungle and into the cool pine forest. We rode all day to Ocosingo, but the cooler temperatures and a slight rain made it pleasant.

On the way into town, a group of kids on bikes started racing us. Usually they would sprint past us, become out of breath and then stop and watch us ride by them. The kids in Chiapas were different. Living in an extremely mountainous area, they were strong. One of the boys who looked about twelve-years old knew how to ride his bicycle. He had another boy, who looked about nine-years old, standing on foot pegs on the back of his bicycle. This made the contest even because of the extra weight of our gear. This kid never tired out. On the downhill into town, we passed him, but he didn't give up. Just before we pulled over to buy gasoline for our stove, he caught me, drafted for a while to rest up, and then sprinted around to victory. I told the gas station attendant the story, and he said that he wasn't surprised. He said, "Mexicans are strong, but more importantly they have heart. Heart will always beat expensive bikes." I agreed with him and pedaled off to Ocosingo to look for a room.

Ocosingo is on the Gringo Trail; however, most tourists don't stop and visit. They simply roar through on their buses. We noticed that most people in town were indigenous and dressed accordingly. The women wore brightly-colored long dresses that were immaculately clean. The men dressed more modernly, but with more worn-out clothes and tattered straw hats. They seldom had shoes on. I wanted to take pictures, but I didn't feel comfortable pulling our camera out around such poverty.

We liked Ocosingo so much that we stayed for nearly a week. We went twice to the nearby Mayan ruins of Tonina and observed the large Mexican festival called Day of the Dead.

On our first visit to the ruins of Tonina, it rained all day. This didn't stop Cindie from marveling at everything. She explored the dark labyrinth located inside one of the temples with a flashlight and studied every stone carving. During our second visit, she did more of the same, and she found a dark narrow stairway leading into the main structure. She was afraid to squeeze down there alone and begged me to lead the way. I will do many things for my wife, but I drew the line here. I didn't think that I would have physically fit, and I didn't like crawling into deep, unstable holes. She had to be satisfied with exploring only the beginning of the passageway.

The Day of the Dead occurs on November 1st and 2nd. The entire family brings food and beer and spends two days partying at the family's section of the graveyard. They decorate the graves with flowers and pictures of popular Catholic saints. Mexican families are big, especially when you count the living and the dead members. It was strange to see everyone so festive in a graveyard. They sat eating and drinking while grandpa told stories about deceased family members. Headstones were used as seats and places to set cans of beer and plates of enchiladas. After I became used to the idea I saw the beauty in the celebration. Death is only another aspect of life and the telling and retelling of stories about loved ones who are gone keeps them alive in family lore. Even though I liked the idea of celebrating death, the Day of the Dead festival was shocking to me.

During our second day walking around the cemetery, the Ramirez family noticed we were strangers and walked up and invited us to their section of the graveyard. We were the only foreigners at the cemetery and stuck out. We were welcomed and made to feel at home. We were introduced to everyone in the family, starting with the dead and progressing from the oldest to the youngest. They cleared the flowers and beer cans away from great grandmother's crypt so we

146

could sit. The next thing I knew I had an open beer in my hand and a huge plate of food in front of me. Once we were settled, Grandpa started telling stories again. His speech was slurred, but it was something about when the family's pigs got loose and how Great Grandma was chasing them around and falling in the mud. During the climax of the story he was laughing so hard he spilled beer and salsa verde all over great uncle Jose's headstone. I politely asked if I could take a few pictures of the family. I wasn't sure if this was considered bad taste because it was in the cemetery. To my delight, they loved the idea and insisted that I get my picture taken with every living member of the family.

We left Ocosingo and the Gringo Trail behind on November 4, 2002 and headed off on a seldom used back country road that climbed deep into indigenous farmland. Our guidebook said this area is poor and contains many Zapatista rebels and supporters. The Zapatista rebels made

Tim celebrating Day of the Dead with the Ramirez family.

international news in 1994 when they emerged from the mountains on horseback fully armed to occupy several key cities, including Ocosingo. The Zapatistas were protesting the Mexican government's policies concerning indigenous rights in Chiapas. The Mexican Army eventually drove them out. The Zapatistas are active today and violence can occur in the area. We saw the Mexican military in force on this road; I wondered how safe this area was for us to ride. In an unstable area like this, the military and rebels could clash, and we could be caught in the crossfire.

Immediately after leaving Ocosingo, we climbed for hours. We passed a large truck that had broken down climbing the steep grade. The occupants were all sitting in the shade waiting for a tow truck, I presumed. During the steepest set of switchbacks, my rear tire slipped on the wet pavement. I worked to keep my bike upright because I knew I couldn't push my bicycle up this steep hill. Cindie struggled to keep her bike going as well. The group of men watched us ride up the hill and cheered us to the top.

After we reached the top, we descended slightly into a picturesque valley. The valley slopes were covered in pine forest. In the middle, sweeping green meadows were covered with sweet smelling grass cut short by grazing animals. It looked like a natural golf course. There were lakes and springs bubbling up from the ground.

The men who tended these animals were barefoot with their pant legs rolled up to mid-calf; they wore round straw hats. They were friendly and waved to us even if they were far away.

We were tired and needed to find a place to camp. We pushed our bikes through a gate to the middle of a grassy field. This was a picturesque and peaceful place to camp. I went in search of water while Cindie pitched the tent. I heard the roar of water and searched for it. I descended into a limestone sinkhole and found a cave. When I was growing up in Indiana, I used to explore the numerous caves there. From the sound of the echo that the water produced, I knew the cave was big and probably went on for miles.

That night was actually cold and we slept well in our sleeping bags.

In the morning, we reluctantly packed for another day on the road. When we were ready to leave, several men came walking by on their way to tend their grazing animals. We didn't hear them approach because they were barefoot. They all had friendly expressions on their face, and I never felt threatened. We had trouble communicating because they didn't speak much Spanish. Their ancient language sounds similar to the Navajo of northeastern Arizona. One of the older men casually tried to pick up my bike to see how heavy it was. He had to reposition himself and get a better hold to get it a few inches off the ground. After that, everyone had to try it. The younger men of the group lifted it as if it weighed nothing. I couldn't believe how strong they were. Life on the farm must be hard work, but it made them healthy and strong. One of them spoke some Spanish and invited us to their ranch for dinner. Sadly, we had to decline because we had to cross the border soon because our Tourist Visa was running out.

We had a delightful ride through the rest of the valley then climbed over a small pass and descended to Comitan, Mexico.

Last Ride in Mexico

November 7, 2002 was our last ride in Mexico, and we rode for 87 kilometers (54 miles). We descended from the high cool mountains back to sea level and the hot, humid tropical jungle. We didn't want to be in the jungle again so soon. It had taken us four days to ride out of the hot lowlands to reach the cool pine forest, but we lost all of that elevation by coasting for an hour. We were lucky this time; the weather

149

was cloudy all day. Without the blazing sun beating down on us, the heat was manageable. We made the border in one day instead of two as we had expected.

Our only break was a truck stop for lunch. This was a muddy place where people waited for the bus from a nearby village and truck drivers rested. This combination restaurant and convenience store had a satellite dish. Everyone was gathered around the TV watching Scooby Doo on the US Boomerang cartoon channel. This wasn't a bunch of kids watching cartoons, but rather a gritty group of men taking a break from their duties as professional truck drivers. Because they were glued to the TV, they barely acknowledged us as we sat down.

During a commercial, we started an interesting conversation about the road to the border and their views on Mexican politics. They explained their views on Guatemala, the border and the problems that they have with Guatemalan citizens illegally sneaking into Mexico to work. We learned that Mexicans earn several times more than their neighbors in Guatemala do. One man in muddy boots and a well-worn hat said, "Thousands of Guatemalan men enter our country, take our jobs, drive wages down and take food from our children's mouths." They also complained about how the stream of illegal aliens created crime problems for Mexicans living near the border zone. They all had much to say on this topic and became emotional and animated during their turns in the conversation. I couldn't help but remember having this same conversation with an American rancher living near the Mexican border. The only thing that was different was the nationality being complained about and the language of the conversation. This was bizarre to me. I had thought that people only were sneaking into the USA to work.

<u>Crossing the Line</u>

At the border, we feared the infamous Latin American bureaucracy. We prepared for this day by wearing our clean clothes, and I got a short haircut. Clean is a relevant concept on the road. We fully expected to be interrogated, searched and forced to pay various fines, fees and kickbacks.

First, we had to get our exit stamp out of Mexico. We couldn't enter Guatemala without it. This required a stop at the Mexican immigration office before actually crossing the border. We rolled our bikes in and had cash ready just in case. We pulled out our yellowing Mexican Tourist cards and the official began to count the days. Even though we had calculated it several times ourselves, we were still nervous. He smiled and told us that we had barely made it. We had been in Mexico 179 days of the 180 days allowed. He vigorously stamped our passports and began photo copying, stapling and signing everything. Wow, that went well, but the real test came next.

It was difficult to say good-bye to Mexico. This had been a good first country to introduce us to the rest of Latin America. The best part of Mexico was the Mexicans themselves. They had been kind, generous and always willing to take the time to help a couple of lost bike tourists find their way or just shoot the breeze.

We had spent more time sleeping in our tent in Mexico than we had anticipated. At first, we had been afraid to camp in this exotic country, but we quickly had become comfortable with the idea. We learned, when we heard a noise outside our tent not to think the worst, but instead expected to find curious children waiting for us to wake. We promised each other to return to Mexico some day. We rode on to the Guatemalan border.

Locals on horseback.

Tim crossing the border from Mexico to Guatemala.

9 Guatemala: Exotic Cultures, Volcanoes and Fireworks

(November 8 - 17, 2002)

The Guatemalan border consisted of a flimsy wooden gate that a guard, with his ancient rifle, would lift after cars were searched and papers checked. I told Cindie, "Smile no matter what." We rode up to the gate with our passports. The guard asked us if we had been checked in and our passports stamped. We answered no, and he pointed to a small shack that was falling apart.

Cindie watched the bikes while I walked past several people helplessly being searched by an immigration officer and then into the shack. I had visions of a lonely stool and a bare light bulb dangling above my head.

A large man (rare in this part of the world) in a tattered blue uniform started asking me questions in a new accent, but still in Spanish. I handed him both of our passports. I had to work at understanding him, but I got most of it. "What is the nature of your visit to Guatemala?" "Do you have guns or drugs on your bodies or in your bike bags?" (He could see Cindie and our bikes through the window). "How long do you wish to be in Guatemala?" This last question was the one I worried about the most. Most tourists get thirty days and a few get sixty days if they ask nicely, but you had to have a good reason to request ninety days. I remembered how I had hated the necessity of a schedule in order to get out of Mexico in time. Guatemala isn't a large country, but there is a lot to see and to do. Only sixty days would be cutting it close, so I wanted ninety days. Three months would mean the freedom to leisurely ride through without a thought to time or schedules. I immediately told him that I was a tourist and certainly didn't have a gun or drugs in my possession.

I pulled out our printed flyer that explains our seven-year travel plans in English and Spanish. He read it carefully and then looked out the window to see our loaded bikes and Cindie perpetually smiling and surrounded by money changers, con men, guards itching to search our stuff and kids begging for money.

I then moved in for the big prize. I said, "Sir, we are traveling by bicycles, and we move slowly. Your beautiful country is vast and contains the largest mountains in Central America. I would like permission to travel in Guatemala for ninety days - PLEASE."

He read our flyer again and thought silently for what seemed like forever. He put down the worn out thirty-day rubber stamp and went to the back room. He returned with a small cardboard box with a picture of a stamp on the side of it and a large "90" written by hand in black marker. It looked brand new even though I knew it wasn't. He happily stamped both of our passports and asked if he could keep the flyer that I had handed him.

Then, to my surprise, he told the guards that no search was necessary, and we could pass.

I knew, from reading our guidebook, that there were no banks in this small border town. I asked the official what a good exchange rate was for US dollars and Mexican pesos to Guatemalan quetzals. He clearly wrote it on a piece of official looking letterhead and told me to accept nothing less. I thanked him, walked out and told the cluster that had gathered around Cindie to get lost. I asked the least obnoxious money changer what the exchange rate was for US dollars to Guatemalan quetzals. He replied with a number much less than what the official had written down for me. I pulled out the paper with the fair rate on it and told the fast-talking man "nothing less." He had a look of defeat and asked me how much I would like to exchange and of what currencies. Cindie then took over. She pays more attention to details like counting money and calculating exchange rates. She exchanged a familiar green US$50 dollar bill first and then our last remaining one hundred Mexican pesos. She was good. She had her calculator and the paper with the fair exchange rates laid out on the back of her load like it was her desk. She went through every calculation with the humbled money changer, and I knew she got it right. I shook hands with the man, and we rode through the opened gate. As we rode away, I distinctly overheard the words "Seven years" and "Are they going to try to ride over THE PASS?" I wondered what PASS they were discussing. Only time would tell.

Out Of the Frying Pan and Into the Fire

The second biggest problem after crossing the border is that now we were in a border town. I am not sure why, but something about towns near international boundaries make them seedy. This seediness goes beyond money changers and drifters traveling north and south. As we cautiously rode from the gate, men and boys would call out to us in broken English: "Hey mister - one green dollar, what you name, you want girl" and so on. We were suspicious of men who only learned a few buzzwords in English. We immediately noticed that all the windows had steel bars and most of the rooftops were barricaded with military style barb wire and attack dogs. It was getting uncomfortably close to sun down. We stopped at a hotel and Cindie went in to check it out. I am not sure what happened in there, but she stormed out with a pale queasy look on her face. I asked her what had happened and she said, "There is absolutely no way I am staying there. I nearly threw up after smelling the bathroom." We went on to an overpriced hotel suggested in our guidebook.

The next day we had only one thing on our minds: We wanted to ride as far from the border as possible. We hoped that Guatemala was much better than what we had expe-

Old American school bus repainted Guatemalan style.

rienced so far. Logic told us that conditions would improve after we left the border zone and entered the real Guatemala. Riding out of town, I couldn't stop thinking, "What have I gotten us into?"

Poverty

On that long ride away from the border, we saw some of the most stunning scenery and overwhelming poverty to date. The images of the extreme poverty that we rode by were shocking and disturbing. Right from the start, we rode past a big trash dump and saw entire families picking through the smelly rotting heap looking for anything to eat or sell. Seeing filthy toddlers playing in the rancid trash made us both feel lucky and guilty for our positions in life. I wondered what could possibly be thrown away of worth in such a poor region.

We paraded past similar scenes with alarming regularity. Extreme poverty was the norm of this area. A few days

156

later, once we were safely in a hotel room in Huehuetenango, Cindie would reflect on the poverty with great distress. She had to keep it together on the road, but in our private room the scenes of the previous few days were flooding her mind, and they haunted her. As she was crying, she said something that I considered profound: "I realize now that seeing the world isn't only looking at the pretty places."

To me this sums it up. To understand the world you have to experience it for better or worse. Traveling by bicycle allows or forces us to see it all. The good, the bad, and the ugly. We cannot avoid things that we would rather not see and are unable to deny their existence. Instead, we slowly experience and absorb everything, whether it's comfortable or not. To ride the bus from one Gringo Island to another would be much easier, but then what would we learn? Certainly not the whole picture of such a complex society with extremes in cultural differences. Therefore, the world isn't only the pretty places. It's often full of misery and hopelessness. As such, our journey isn't always easy or even fun. Nothing this educational and enlightening could be. I truly think it will be worth it in the end; however, I sometimes cannot help wondering if I am crazy during the hard times. I am learning about the world but at what cost? The answer may be our innocence.

The Long Ride Up From The Border

We had yet another five thousand foot climb ahead of us. We were getting stronger again; however, we knew that we would never make it up this mountain in one day.

To start, we rode for hours in a deep and narrow canyon. For dozens of slow kilometers there was barely enough room for our narrow two-lane road and the raging mountain river. Level land was scarce and every bit of it was used for small crops and simple houses. Many places on the high canyon walls were dug out by hand and terrace farmed. I was in awe watching strong women cling to the cliffs while tend-

157

ing crops. From a distance, they appeared to defy gravity. Once we were closer, we saw that they were barefoot and usually carried babies in colorful hand woven blankets over their backs.

While we were resting and eating our tortilla and avocado sandwiches a man descended from a steep trail in the canyon wall. He wasn't surprised to see foreigners on loaded bicycles resting on his trail. He was barefoot and hadn't anything with him but torn clothing, a faded hat and a continuous smile. He calmly and matter of factly walked up to me and asked me what my name was. I answered with my Spanish name "Timatao," and I asked him what his name was. He answered "Moses." Moses didn't ask us about our travel plans or where we were from. He already seemed to know. Moses told us of the wonderful things that we could expect on the road in his country. He told us that we were going to have a fine time in Guatemala and, although there would be excitement, we would cross into Honduras wiser and unharmed. It was eerie, because he was dead sure about it. How did he know that we were going to Honduras? The logical guess would have been to El Salvador. Most travelers take that well-beaten route. Bizarre! He bid us farewell and shook my hand with both of his. He walked off to an unknown destination seemingly without a care in the world.

The thought of camping so soon in a new and different country was scary, but it was getting late and looked like rain. We found a spring and collected our usual ten liters (2.6 gallons) of water to filter later. Tying twenty pounds of sloshing water to my bike already loaded down with several days of food and our abundant gear is never appealing. Always, the plan is to find a suitable place to camp as soon as possible. As the skies turned darker and the wind picked up, we knew time was short. We rode kilometer after kilometer, but there was no semi-level ground. Hiding from the road was starting to look unlikely as well.

Exotic Cultures, Volcanoes and Fireworks

Fruit Bombs

As I was toting the heavy water bag and desperately looking for anyplace to sleep we heard something hit the road, SPLAT! My first thought was that a rock had rolled down from above, or worse, a landslide was about to happen. Little did I know that it was much worse than either one of these two scenarios.

Next, we heard SPLAT SPLAT and then saw with terror that large pieces of fruit were hitting the road. Somebody high above us was purposely throwing something about the size and weight of a cantaloupe at us. They threw it from at least 200 feet (61 meters) above us, and we both instantly knew that if something that heavy thrown from that height hit us we could easily be killed. I looked up and saw nothing but towering cliffs. I yelled, "Let's get out of here" and the sprint for our lives was on. I was slow to pick up speed because of the awkward weight of the water strapped on back.

Cindie bolted past me and instinctively headed for a rock overhang seventy feet (five meters) away. SPLAT SPLAT! Their aim was improving; the fruit hit only a meter away from me. Unfortunately I was wearing a bright orange jersey; I must have made a big and inviting target. Then they were throwing their fruit bombs in groups of two and three. I thought, "Who in this area has food to waste?" Simultaneously one hit off my front left side and then directly in front of me. My rear wheel spun out on the slick flesh of the melon as I rode through the spray. I almost crashed. I knew if I did, I would give them ample time to hit their mark. I kept the bike upright and made it to the overhang. We were both shaken but kept riding. We were worried that someone with a bag of melons was running along an unknown trail to get to the next throwing position.

It started to rain, and we still had no place to camp. We picked up our pace and became less picky about where we

159

would pitch the tent. The thought of camping in the open knowing that there were people crazy enough to try to kill us with melon bombs gave us an uneasy feeling. Cindie was scared to stop so close to the area where we had been attacked. Several times, I thought I saw a passable place, but upon closer inspection found that it was too small or it was a big drop off. We were still in the narrow canyon. Gone was any notion that we would be able to hide for the night. The rain was steadily picking up its pace. Finally, after several kilometers of frantic searching, a roof appeared. At first, I thought it was someone's house, but a sign on it stated that it was a municipally-owned bus stop. The rock foundation was high enough to be out of the mud and the tin roof more or less worked.

At that moment, the rain tripled its pace and began coming down in sheets. We rolled in not believing our luck. The best thing was that the traffic's headlights didn't reveal us as they rounded the bend in the road. We were hoping that once it was completely dark and we remained motionless no one would see us. Of course, to achieve this level of secrecy we couldn't pitch the tent. After the melons, we didn't know what to expect. I kept the only things that come close to weapons in my hands all night. I was armed with a large, but not fierce looking, Swiss Army Knife and a flashlight to shine in my attacker's eyes. I slept little that night. As I lay awake listening to Cindie snoring and the rain hammering the thin roof above us, I wondered what was next.

The rain had stopped, and I saw the sunrise over the misty mountain. Everything was still and peaceful. I woke and started boiling water for coffee. Then the silence was broken. Dozens of indigenous people descended down from the villages on twisting steep trails. I quickly hid our short-wave radio and went about my business of boiling water. I didn't think these humble people wanted to rob us, but I have never thought that showing expensive things to these

Our first campsite in Guatemala, a bus stop.

extremely poor people is right. To my surprise, they were
interested in our camp stove. They asked many questions
in a local indigenous language, not in Spanish. Finally, they
brought a boy forward who went to school and spoke fluent
Spanish. Few had the privilege of education in this community. They were respectful of our space, orderly and polite.
They wanted to know what the stove burned (gasoline), how
long a liter (0.26 gallons) of gasoline lasted (five days at two
meals a day) and how much the stove cost (750 quetzales or
US$100). Through the translator, we learned that, for them,
cooking involved hours of collecting firewood every week.

Many members of the village made their meager living
by gathering large, heavy bundles of firewood and carrying
it up to ten kilometers (six miles) into a city and to sell it to
restaurants and private homes. It would take a good eight
to twelve hours to sell all that they could carry. Depending
on how much they could carry, they made eight to fifteen
quetzals (about US$1 to US$2) a day. A liter (0.26 gallons) of

gasoline cost less than US$0.50. The crowd quickly became divided about the use of such a stove. Someone said that if they had a gasoline stove they could use it in the house and not burn wood that could be sold. They asked me to demonstrate how it was lit and how it worked in general. They marveled at its convenience. Building fires and cleaning up the ash is time consuming. Others pointed out that if a gasoline stove became popular then there would be no market for their firewood. If they couldn't sell firewood, how would they feed their children? The friendly debate went on without being translated to us.

I have no idea what their conclusion was, but I will never use our stove in the presence of such poverty again. We have a lot to learn about conducting ourselves among poverty. We also decided to take our gold wedding rings off and stash them until we entered a less desperate area. We removed our wedding rings not because we feared being robbed, but to avoid unwanted attention and being showy.

The last forty-eight kilometers (thirty miles) to our first real city in Guatemala was almost entirely uphill. The road rose gently; the higher we rode the cooler, and more pleasant the weather became. It was also obvious that we had broken free of the border zone. The transient movements of desperate people and the feeling that some were trying to cheat us was gone. Most people weren't rich, but they looked content with life. People were friendly and helpful. We finally felt like riding through Guatemala would be possible. We still rode through pockets of intense poverty, but we were getting used to it – as used to it as is possible, I guess.

Huehuetenango

By the time we rolled into Huehuetenango, we were exhausted. We had climbed more than five thousand feet (1,525 meters) into thinning air and experienced a range of emotions along the way. We found a room, took a shower and relaxed in the safety of our four walls. We stayed in

Huehuetenango for several days. We used the time to get our clothes washed and collect information on Guatemala and the road ahead.

We met an American man, Mike, married to a Guatemalan woman, who had lived in Huehuetenango for years. He looked to be in his late 50's. He was an animated man and became excited as he told us his views of the recent civil war and current Guatemalan politics. He spoke loudly in the crowded internet cafe and openly aired his complaints about the Guatemalan government and the current president Alfonso Portillo. Although few people in the crowded room understood English, most had worried looks on their faces every time he loudly said the president's name. This made me uneasy. From the reaction of the people around us in the internet cafe, I didn't think that it was healthy to criticize the Guatemalan president publicly.

Mike was particularly vocal about the civil war that ended only six years before. This terrible and hard to understand war had lasted for over thirty years. Mike told us that Huehuetenango was in the heart of the conflict and had experienced extreme violence and carnage. "In the dark days of the war Huehuetenango was practically a ghost town and was called the valley of death because people were disappearing every day." Mike said that the government army created death squads that had a genocidal goal of wiping out the indigenous poor. Mike accused the death squads of killing randomly and even going into indigenous villages and killing every inhabitant.

I didn't get to know Mike well, but I think that he was prone to exaggerating the facts and even making things up. In his defense, several books support his views on the war. Other books dispute these extreme views. I take no sides in this debate, but it's clear to me that the people in this area had been through a lot. We encountered unmistakable nervousness and caution in the local people that we met.

163

Many Guatemalan people in Huehuetenango told us not to go out after dark except to the main plaza and even there not too late.

Through The Forest

We left Huehuetenango well rested and more informed on what to expect, but we continued to encounter the unexpected. We came face-to-face with two rumors during our long three-day climb deep into the highlands. First, we were told that the local children were frightened of us. Second, many people told us about a rumor that was persistently circulated among the indigenous groups in this area: they believed that foreigners, particularly white women, were stealing babies presumably to be sold for adoption in the wealthy nations of the world. At first, the thought of these hard working people thinking this was difficult to believe.

Reality set in a few kilometers out of Huehuetenango. We were slowly climbing at six kilometers per hour (four miles per hour) when we rounded a corner and gradually caught up with young girls herding their goats across the road. They took one look at us, dropped all of their possessions, and ran for their lives. In their haste, they left their goats in the road in danger of being killed by traffic. We didn't know what to do. I knew that the milk, meat and revenue generated by these goats, was likely the only thing that stood between these people and starvation.

Do we get off our bikes and move the goats off the road? Do we try to show them that we don't wish to harm them?

The thought of the girls returning with their father and his rifle (left over from the civil war) kept us moving. If we had stopped to move the goats off the road, they would have surely thought we were attacking them. We hurried to get around the next bend and out of sight in hopes that they would return to their goats. Although traffic was light the Guatemalan bus drivers are notoriously known to take chances and drive fast. We never looked back, and we didn't see any traffic pass us. I would like to believe that the girls collected the herd and returned to their lives.

Several miles later, we rode past a mother who was collecting water from a spring near the side of the road. We moved as far to the center of the road as safety would allow. Because we quietly approached on bicycles, we were upon her before she knew it. She was scared out of her mind. We both saw her cover her baby with her wrap and physically tremble in uncontrollable fear.

Neither of us had signed on for this adventure to scare little girls and young mothers. Similar incidents happened every dozen kilometers or so, and it ate at my conscience. I started to wonder if foreigners had been stealing their babies. There certainly is a large, illegal and lucrative market in the world for infant babies. I have always believed that if there is a way to make money then there is somebody out there making it. I am guessing that indigenous babies are probably born in their houses without a birth certificate or other documentation. If they are missing, there probably isn't much recourse for the family.

This was the first time the locals had been afraid of us. Seeing the fear in the locals made us feel like we were intruding.

We climbed for days in the crisp mountain air until we reached the top of a 9,500 feet (2,898 meters) pass. We collected water from a village well, rode our bikes for two kilometers (1.3 miles) and then pushed our bikes into the forest to a hidden place that we thought was peaceful. The altitude made it cold. We pitched the tent while listening to Radio Canada International on the shortwave radio. Just then, ten kids and an old man came walking through the forest. I turned the radio off and quickly covered it and the stove from view. As soon as they saw the tent, they approached. When

I stood to greet them, all of the girls and the younger boys immediately ran away in fear of me, "the pale giant." A few older boys walked up first, but said nothing to us until the old man arrived. Respect for elders appeared to be important in this culture. He was obviously in charge of the kids. The older boys were comfortable with us and eager to get to know us. Other than my repeated friendly Spanish greetings the silence was broken only when the old man spoke. He was only five feet (1.53 meters) tall, but had the look of surviving decades of violence and the wisdom that comes with age. He spoke a choppy dialect that we didn't understand. One thing was certain. It was a different language than we had heard on the lower slopes of this three-day climb.

Seeing that we didn't understand him, the old man switched over to Spanish. He kept his distance and was obviously afraid of us. I noticed that his hands trembled as he held his machete, still sheathed, tightly in his grip. I sat back down to present a nonviolent posture that put him more at ease. His questions were focused on finding out what we were doing camped near his village. I told him that we were peaceful bicycle travelers only passing through. He examined our bikes and looked in our tent. Although there is no way to be certain, I believe he was looking for stolen babies or other evidence of bad intentions. He asked, "Do you and your wife have children?" I thought it best to lie. I told him that we did and even ran through their names and ages. Satisfied that we weren't stealing babies he reverted to asking us about our travels. He finally approached close enough to shake my hand and wish us good travels.

As a parting remark, he warned us that it was dangerous to camp there. When I asked what he meant by this he said, "There are many bad men on the road at night that have guns and no respect for peaceful people." He bid us good luck and walked to the unknown village.

Exotic Cultures, Volcanoes and Fireworks

As darkness fell, we quietly sat and contemplated our chances of making it through the night. To put the old man's warning into perspective we remembered that he had seen over thirty years of war. In this war he had probably seen many close friends and family members killed. His fear and paranoia was understandable. On the other hand, we thought, what if he was talking about some other real and current danger.

I endured another sleepless night. I never zipped up my sleeping bag even though it was cold. I kept my shoes on and my worthless weapons in hand. It was too cold for mosquitoes so I kept the tent door open as well. I wanted to be able to get out and be ready to go if necessary. I heard many noises during the night, which I regularly investigated and found nothing. The warning from the weathered old man ran repeatedly in my brain. I don't think that Cindie slept either. Morning broke slowly in the dense forest and we crawled out of the tent. Another false alarm or another dangerous night passed uneventfully.

With our nerves calmed, we started our morning routine. We made coffee and oatmeal, listened to FM radio, and slowly packed all of our gear on our human powered machines. We saw women in the distance gathering pine needles into huge bundles. As usual with indigenous women, they had infants on their backs. I predicted that they would keep their distance, but to our surprise, they worked their way close to us. They greeted us and didn't appear to be afraid. The old man must have told them that we were OK. We learned quickly in the Guatemalan Highlands not to look at or otherwise acknowledge the babies. Eventually all their work was stopped and we were engaged in a friendly conversation. Everyone was introduced, including the babies. We talked about how beautiful the forest was and how lucky they were to live there. They were interested in our camp chairs and the material of our bike shorts. It was nice not to scare the highland villagers.

Traveling Back In Time

We were nearly packed when one of the women in the curious group invited us to her house in the village for lunch. She introduced herself as Maria. This was an incredible opportunity and impossible to pass up. We felt that it would be rude to turn down her offer. They loaded their heavy bundles of pine needles on their backs with babies on the front and insisted that we follow. They went down a trail that descended quickly into a remote valley. It was so steep and muddy I could barely ride down it; walking the heavy loaded bike would have been impossible. If this hadn't been such a rare opportunity to see life in a hidden world, I would have said that the trail was impossible. Returning up the hill promised to be even more difficult.

Once we reached the floor of the small valley, it was as if we traveled back in time. Wells had ropes, cranks and buckets. Girls played with dolls made from corn husks. People thought that a fat pig was about the best thing that you could own. Everyone stared at us as we passed through the village, then an excited group of children were soon following us. I wish that I had understood the unending comments going on around us. At least they seemed to be positive and friendly.

At the end of the village, we rolled our bikes through a cornfield and into Maria's back yard. It was hard not to show our amazement at this fascinating way of life. Cornfields surrounded her dirt floor house with no electricity or running water. Water had to be brought to the house in buckets from the village well a kilometer away. All of their clothing was handmade, brightly colored and perfectly clean. I also saw a wash basin with what looked like homemade soap. It was obvious that they made or grew everything they used.

Maria asked how far we had to carry water from the well to our house. I answered that we didn't have to carry water far but that wells in Arizona were deep. I tried to explain to them about the dryness of the desert, but I could tell that they didn't believe that such a place existed. Another woman asked what we grew in our fields. We liberally translated this to vegetables Cindie grew in her small garden back in Prescott, Arizona. Someone asked if our homeland was currently at war or peace. At first, I thought this was a funny question because war, as these people knew it, was unthinkable in Arizona. Then I considered Afghanistan and possibly Iraq and concluded to myself that while Americans aren't threatened in the same ways as these villagers are, the people that we are dropping bombs on certainly were. I thought a long time before I answered her troubling question. I told her that we currently have war, but the battle was far from our house. She said that she thought the war was far from her house until surprisingly the killing came to her village. She even said something about violence arriving at her front door. There was an extreme air of sadness, and I changed the subject. What secrets and horrors these people must keep inside to continue with life.

Maria went to the field and picked several ears of corn. She cut the kernels from the cob and boiled them in water. This was our drink. We were glad that the water was boiled because we were certain it would give us stomach problems otherwise. Next, she roasted ears of corn on the fire and gave it to us. They were good. The roasted ears of corn tasted a lot like popcorn. I believed that corn was a major part of their diet.

It was time to say good-bye we gave them a bag of peanuts as a parting gift. They accepted the gift enthusiastically. I could tell that they seldom get something different to eat or anything that was purchased from a store.

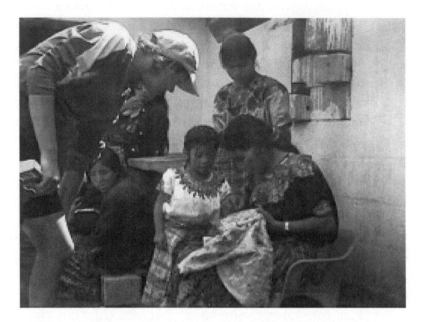

Cindie looking closely at a handmade blouse.

Cindie with Maria and her family.

We slowly pushed our bikes back up the trail and back to the paved road. Getting up the slick wet trail was difficult because I couldn't ride up the steep muddy hill. One of the local boys helped me push my bike up the trail. I wouldn't have made it without his help. I was unable to thank him properly because we spoke no common language. Cindie pushed her bike as far as she could and waited for me to come back and help her push her bike to the top of the muddy hill.

The rest of the ride to Quetzaltenango was pleasant because of the cool air and light traffic. We descended several kilometers from the pass and soon found ourselves in Quetzaltenango's main plaza. Wow, we made it!

Cindie pushing her bike through a cornfield from Maria's house.

Tim fixing a flat.

Cindie walking through Quetzaltenango.

10 From Paradise to Despair

(November 17 - January 6, 2003)

We stayed in Quetzaltenango, the second largest city in Guatemala, while Cindie went to another Spanish school. While we were there, we went on several day trips with students from the Spanish school. We climbed the Volcano Santa Maria and visited several nearby Mayan villages.

One weekend morning we woke up at 4:00 a.m. to meet everyone at the school to take a taxi to the base of the volcano Santa Maria.

The climb up the volcano started out slow, and we passed many cornfields on the lower slope of the volcano. The climb began to get steep, and it stayed steep. In areas, the trail was muddy and slippery. At one point, I was hanging from a root trying to get a grip and climb up to the trail. I carried most of our water, 7.5 liters (two gallons) and food.

Climbing to the top of a volcano was different from climbing to the top of a mountain. Unlike a mountain with a summit, we went up a ridge straight to the top of the volcano. The group from the Utitlan Spanish School was waiting for us at the top. While we were eating lunch, we watched a nearby volcano, Santiaguito erupt. An excellent display of the forces of nature!

Thanksgiving in Quetzaltenango

Thanksgiving in Quetzaltenango was different from what we were used to in the USA. We went to the only advertised Thanksgiving dinner in the city. It was proudly listed as vegetarian. It turned out that it was all of the usual Thanksgiving foods minus the turkey. A local woman who had lived in Chicago for ten years cooked the meal. It was surprisingly traditional except for the lack of a turkey.

Volcano Santiaguito erupting.

At dinner, we met about every American in town, maybe twelve in all. Thanksgiving is an American holiday after all. It was great to hear English spoken in an accent not unlike my own.

For a country of 280 million, there are few Americans traveling abroad. We easily met more Canadians and Dutch (people from Holland) than citizens of the USA. These two countries only have a small fraction of the USA's population. Americans even have the shortest distance to travel to Guatemala. I consider this a disturbing fact because the USA is extremely involved or in the forefront of world politics, but its people experience so little of the world. I am certain that we have bombed countries that many USA citizens cannot find on a world map. After a long talk with a Dutch friend in Guatemala, we came to a few informal conclusions of our own. Politically, the world would be a much different place if Americans traveled internationally or at least paid more attention to world politics. Americans generally don't know much about other countries, and the people from around the world don't usually understand Americans because they never meet them. They experience Americans and their way of life only through television and films. I found that foreigners tend to think that attitudes of the American people are the same as the US government. We are seen as arrogant and pushy. I explained to my Dutch friend that our government is involved in things that most Americans don't know about. This isn't because it's a big secret, but instead because we are content and aren't aware of the outside world. I believe that travel is the cure for this problem. Americans generally have two weeks of vacation a year -or less- and it's not practical to leave the country for such a short time frame. I believe if Americans had the same four to eight weeks annual vacation that Europeans do, we would travel the globe more and be more aware of international politics.

Stories and Warnings of Crime

Quetzaltenango was our first place in Guatemala that had an abundance of foreign travelers. Many were heading to Mexico and had recently traveled through the areas that we were soon going. This gave us a chance to hear stories and descriptions about what lay ahead. This is when we started hearing firsthand accounts of people being robbed and worse all over Guatemala.

We didn't meet many people who were robbed in Mexico. Guatemala was another reality. We actually met the victims of crimes in Guatemala. Some were pick pocketed in crowded markets or on the street. Experienced travelers never carry valuables in a pant or jacket pocket. Another common scenario was using razor blades to slice through backpack pockets on crowded buses or even completely cutting a camera or purse strap and running off with it. Even well informed travelers have to board crowded buses or walk around town with their backpacks. I am not sure what preventive measure they employ, but they must have a strategy. I read that this type of petty crime occurs all over the world and especially in crowded bus or train stations where foreign tourists are present. We avoided most of these types of problems by traveling by bicycle and not using public transportation. I also believe that the thieves weren't familiar with the types of luggage that a bike tourist uses. Cindie stashed money in her bike shoe and in two different panniers on her bike. We came up with what we call the dummy wallet. It had expired credit cards, old driver's licenses and a small amount of money we used on a daily basis. If that wallet were stolen, we would only lose a small amount of cash and no valuable documents. We felt better knowing that all our money wasn't in one place. There were also the stories of violent crime in Guatemala involving the use of guns or knives. This is what concerned me the most.

We started seeking more information to establish a pattern. We found the US Embassy's Web site and their chilling list of crimes committed against foreigners. We decided that there were things that we could do to decrease the risk including avoiding isolation. There was a road that we had planned on riding but decided against it after reading that it was a regular place for highway bandits to stop traffic and rob people. This wasn't a main road but an attractive shortcut between Lake Atitlan and Antigua. It was probably a road with little traffic. Highway crime would be difficult with a constant flow of traffic. Therefore, we concluded that we didn't want to take lonely roads in this country. In fact being isolated in any way was a bad idea. It was also common to rob tourists on quiet trails while they were hiking.

Down the Road Again: Our Highest Point Yet

We left Quetzaltenango on the Pan American Highway and immediately began to climb. It was a pleasant day and this road, built to international standards, never was too steep. As we climbed to over nine thousand feet (2,745 meters), the air grew crisp and we soon put on our long-sleeve jerseys.

At the end of the day, we collected water from a village well and found a hidden place to set up our tent. We spent the evening cooking dinner while watching the sunset in this exotic land. We had found one of those near perfect places to camp; it was flat and well hidden from the road. We weren't close enough to the road to be awakened by traffic noise. However, we could still smell the burning brake pads of overcrowded buses that had been descending for dozens of miles. From our camp chairs, we looked deep into the valley below to see tiny villages and their surrounding fields. We could also look up to see a wall of mountains that we still had to climb.

Visitors to Our Camp

Just before the sun was completely down, three men carrying various farm tools walked through camp. They had no women or children with them and weren't afraid of us. This was a welcome change from most of the initial encounters of the past few weeks.

They were happy and excited to see us sitting next to their trail. They acted as if we were long lost friends. They had big smiles when they introduced themselves one by one. "I am Antonio from the village of something?-Tenango," said one of the men with his hand extended to shake. As the others ran through their names and villages, I stood up to show respect. When I did this, their eyes opened wider, and they all nervously stepped back. It was obvious that my large size (6'4", 1.93 meters) intimidated them. I put on my biggest and friendliest smile while extending my hand to shake. This is my international symbol of nonaggression, and it has always worked in the past.

They looked at each other, nodded, and stepped forward to all shake my hand and nod at Cindie who was sitting in her camp chair quietly watching our exchange. The ice had been broken. They were all smiles again and asked a million questions.

I wanted to know about their daily lives, what the tools in their hands were for and what they did for fun. They would have nothing of it. They wanted to know about us. After answering the usual questions of where we were from

Our campsite where we were visited by locals.

and why we were traveling by bicycles, they asked us some funny questions. They asked, how many ears of corn can you eat for dinner and did we have to build a special large house for me to fit in? I must have looked like a freak of nature to them.

When they saw that it was getting dark, they bid us farewell. People in the Guatemalan highlands liked to be home before dark. I wondered if this was a legacy of the recent civil war.

In the morning, after heating my coffee water and putting the stove away, the three men were again smiling before me. This time they had brought their families with them. Obviously, they stopped by to see us. There were about fifteen people in all. They were dressed in heavy, layered clothing, which tells a story of a hard life at high altitude and in cold weather. The women's dresses were colorful and handmade. We later learned that the specific design and colors represented the village in which they lived. The sons stayed with their fathers while the girls kept close to their mothers and cautiously walked over and looked in the open door of our tent. This time it was the girls with the questions. "Did you sleep here? Were you cold last night?" I talked with the men, and Cindie talked with women as is expected in these indigenous cultures. As quickly as they came, they left, walking down the road to an unknown destination.

We packed and started for the highest point on the Pan American Highway in Central America. Our map indicated that it was well over twelve thousand feet (3,660 meters). We decided that this must be, "The Pass" that people had mentioned at the border.

We climbed for a long time until the road leveled, and we could see a small village in the distance. Two young indigenous boys were walking down the road. They saw us coming and decided to run beside us as we slowly climbed

Tim at the Pass, highest point in Central America.

the hill. We were climbing slightly, but it was the thin air that was slowing us down. They kept up with us for about a half of a kilometer (0.3 miles) until the road finally started to descend. They probably returned home with a story that no one will believe about a bicycle loaded like a burro.

Riding Into a Volcano

After a long descent and several more rolling kilometers, we found ourselves at the turn for Lake Atitlan. This was one of three secondary roads from the Pan America Highway to the lake. Even though this was the least-busy road, we believed that it was the safest. The US Embassy's Web site didn't have any reports of robbery on this road, and it wasn't a road that tourists used because the main road from Antigua to Panajachel was on the other side of the lake.

From Paradise to Despair

Lake Atitlan is actually inside of a large volcano – a caldera as Cindie the Geologist refers to it. Our road to San Pedro de Laguna slowly climbed to the lip of the volcano then descended steeply to the lake. The climb wasn't so bad, but as we climbed the steep part near the top, I couldn't stop thinking about how easy a target we would be for thieves. This road had little traffic. From the curious looks that we received from the people living on small farms, I could tell that not many foreigners used this road. This made me feel better. My thinking was "Why would wolves hunt where there aren't sheep."

From the top, we could barely make out the ring of the volcano because of the clouds. The descent was the longest stretch of steep, tight switchbacks that we had ridden on the trip so far. The route was like the Bright Angel Trail that descends into the Grand Canyon – if it were paved – all the way to the Colorado River. It was so steep and technical that it was absolutely no fun. Our brakes heated so quickly that we had to stop often to cool them by squirting water on them. Our hands ached from the white-knuckle grip that was continuously necessary. This road hadn't anything in the way of guardrails or warning signs. It was a never-ending plunge. At one of our brake cooling stops Cindie reminded me repeatedly that there was no way she was riding back up this hill. I agreed with her and honestly don't think that I would have made it back up either.

We finally arrived at the bottom of the crater on the shore of the lake; we then had to find the village of San Pedro de Laguna. We rode through several isolated villages with indigenous people wearing colorful clothing, speaking a vanishing language and living traditional lives. The locals looked at us in astonishment. I believe that they knew all about the road that we had descended and wondered how we did it.

Catholic church in San Pedro de Laguna.

After asking several people for directions and generally riding around more than our share of villages, we finally arrived in San Pedro de Laguna. While we were sitting in the plaza for a rest, we met a little girl who offered to show us to the part of town with the hotels. I think we took the back way, but she eventually got us to the boat dock. I gave the little girl a quetzal (US$0.13) for her help. It was hard to find a room because several places were full. After all of the work of negotiating the room price and getting our bikes and gear up two flights of stairs we were finally settled. What a day!

San Pedro de Laguna was like heaven on earth. It sits on the shores of the incredible lake Atitlan and has stunning views of the large clear lake and surrounding rim of the caldera. From reading our guidebook, we expected it to be touristy. Instead, it was laid back. It's a place where drifters stop drifting. Many had come for a week and stayed for a decade. It was easy to see why.

San Pedro de Laguna is known by travelers to be the cheapest place on the trail north of the Panama Canal. After spending a week here, I agreed. Cindie and I had a clean but simple room at the Belle Vista Hotel, which offered million dollar views from its communal deck. For our US$3 a night, we even had use of a shared kitchen, which delighted Cindie who missed having two burners at the same time and a sink with running water. A dinner at a restaurant with beefsteak, beans, potatoes, guacamole and tortillas cost under US$2 per person. You can easily eat for much less if you bought food from the open-air market. I calculated that Cindie and I could live comfortably in San Pedro de Laguna on US$500 a month. Most foreign people living there said that we could live there on half that amount. Although it was tempting to drop anchor and stay for several years, we still had a lot of the world to experience and weren't ready to stop yet. For the traveler the curiosity to see what is around the next bend in the road is stronger than the need to be in a familiar comfortable place.

While staying in San Pedro de Laguna we went on a hike along the shore of the lake. Lake Atitlan has dozens of small villages on its shores and an extensive passenger boat service to connect them all. Each village has a different indigenous group with their own distinctive colorful dress and language. The passenger boats are cheap to ride and are the lifeline to the outside world for the various villages along the lake. These villages don't have roads leading to them and therefore have absolutely no cars or motorized traffic.

Besides the boats, there are footpaths that connect each village and this is where we hiked. Our plan was to take a boat to the far end of the lake and walk from one village to another until we were tired and then take a boat back to San Pedro de Laguna. The trails were used by farmers tending their terraced coffee and vegetable fields that cling to the inside of the steep walls of the caldera. This hike had spectacular views at every turn.

Two days later, another foreigner that we met staying in our hotel returned from the exact same hike shaken up. He announced that four local boys about sixteen years old, armed with machetes, robbed him of his money and camera on the deserted trail between villages. Wow, we had been on that exact same trail only forty-eight hours earlier. It

Mayan girls we meet on our hike.

View across Lake Atitlan from San Marcos.

could have easily happened to us, and we would have lost our expensive camera and some money.

Professional Travelers

San Pedro de Laguna was our first glimpse into the world of the professional traveler. Professional travelers, by my personal definition, are those who earn their funds as they drift around from place to place. They network and know where the short-term work is all over the world. They may work in a busy bar on the beach during the high season then travel several months to arrive at harvest time to pick fruit to save up for the next leg of their travels. Another scenario is to circle the globe earning money while performing on the street. We have seen people performing magic acts with a hat out for donations or simply playing guitar on a street corner. The romantic image of drifters with a duffel bag and a guitar slung over their backs is a reality for a large sub-culture of people. This is truly living on the edge and much

185

more adventurous than what Cindie and I were doing. We knew where our next meal was coming from, and we had the option of flying home whenever we'd had enough. A professional traveler has no safety net and faces hardship if things don't go well.

Because San Pedro de Laguna is such an inexpensive place, we met these professional travelers taking a break from their occupations and enjoying the good life on Lake Atitlan. We spent a few days with an adventurous couple, Nacho and Melinda, from the small South American country of Uruguay. Melinda crocheted women's clothes and bikinis and Nacho made jewelry from twisting wire with stones and shells. They were spending a few days in San Pedro before they were off to look for work among the tourist restaurants and bars of Roatan, Honduras. Roatan, a tropical island, is a big stop on the Gringo Trail for diving and Caribbean beaches. An expensive tourist area must have a good labor market with higher than average wages. After Roatan, they weren't sure where they were going next. Nacho mentioned working and selling their crafts in the Mexican beach resort of Cancun. This would be after several weeks of hitchhiking and visiting the Mayan ruins in the area.

Nacho and I both liked getting up early in the morning. We would sit on the hotel's porch to drink coffee and watch the sunrise over the towering wall of the caldera that rings the lake. He spoke Spanish with an accent I had never heard before. He knew to speak slowly and clearly to me and we understood each other well.

They had left home several years before and had traveled slowly north while working in various locations and selling their crafts on the street. We saw their makeshift store one day. They would lay a blanket out and methodically display everything they had to sell. It was an impressive and industrious thing to see. Melinda would crochet quickly while Nacho was negotiating prices and collecting money.

Business looked good. I wondered what Cindie and I could sell on the street but nothing came to mind.

I asked Nacho where the hot spots were to work in the world, in particular South America. He listed what places have a shortage of labor and what time of year is best for finding work. The list was long, and I should have written it down. Professional travelers follow a definite trail in South America as they eventually make their way to Europe or North America. He said that from Brazil to Portugal or Spain is the cheap flight option to Europe. Once on that continent there is a well-beaten trail of temporary work that follows harvest times and peak seasons at resorts that will take you through Europe and beyond.

Festival Celebrating the Virgin Mary

While we were in San Pedro de Laguna, we were lucky enough to see the Fiesta de la Concepcion. This is the Catholic tradition which celebrates the Angel Gabriel's announcement to the Virgin Mary that she is pregnant with the Messiah. In San Pedro de Laguna, the evening of the December 8 mass was held at the Catholic Church and then a procession with the Virgin Mary began.

A statue of the Virgin Mary in traditional Mayan dress was taken from the Church and paraded through the streets for two hours. Firecrackers were lit along the parade route before she arrives. Fireworks increase as the Virgin Mary returns to the church. Before she arrives back at the church, a man crawls inside a wooden bull covered with fireworks; the fireworks are lit, and he runs through the crowd like a crazy man until all the fireworks have gone off. How he survives this ordeal, I don't know.

At the entrance of the church an entire fireworks display is set up and let off before the Virgin Mary returns to the church. I have no idea how fireworks and religious proces-

The Virgin Mary in Mayan dress.

sions have joined in this country, but I haven't found one without the other here.

As we were walking around the village witnessing the festivities, a large group of indigenous women was walking quickly down the street. They approached and engulfed Cindie and me before they passed us and disappeared into the crowd. It was a blur of colorful dresses and gray hair neatly braided down their backs. The few moments that we were in the middle of their group, I realized how small the Mayan women are compared to me. Not one of them was higher than my belt. Local men are only slightly taller than that. I felt like I was a giant that had descended into another world. Doorways and market stalls also match these proportions. The story of "Gulliver's Travels" came back to me. Regularly people asked me how tall I am and they are surprised when I answer nearly two meters (6' 4" feet).

We stayed in San Pedro de Laguna for a week before we got the itch to travel again and decided to move on. The day we left San Pedro de Laguna, we had a mixture of feelings. We were sad to leave such a peaceful place, excited to be back on the road and nervous because the road from Lake Atitlan to the Pan American Highway was notoriously bad for road crime.

We easily had our bikes and gear loaded on the small but fast boat. This boat took us to the tacky tourist town of Panajachel. Panajachel had a bad reputation for crime and even the locals warned us not to go out at night with valuables on us. When the boat pulled up to the dock, we were overwhelmed by what we saw there. Hundreds of stalls selling souvenirs and other useless items lined the streets. Instead of locals sitting in the plaza with us and telling us about their lives, I had to fend off hordes of obnoxious hawkers shoving trinkets in our faces while I kept an eye out for pickpockets, too. I would greet people with "good afternoon" in Spanish, and they would reply in English "How many do you want to buy mister" while they were pointing at a necklace that they were selling. When I replied in silence and confusion, the salesman repeated his pitch in German and then Italian.

It wasn't surprising that the locals looked at us as fools to be separated from our cash. This place was overrun with foreign tourists – so full, in fact, that the Guatemalans in the rest of the country call Panajachel "Gringo-Tenango" (the joke being that most towns in the highlands have "Tenango"

189

at the end of their names and this town had more gringos then indigenous). After looking around, we only wanted to get our loaded bikes into a secure room before the sun went down. Finding an available and secure looking room was a headache. After finding our hotel room, we had a quiet and uneventful night.

After repeated warnings and credible reports of crime on the road out of town, we decided to catch a ride in the back of a pickup to the Pan America highway. This was surprisingly easy. In the morning, we were riding around town, and I saw a pickup truck drop several women off. I rolled up to the driver's window. I told the driver where we wanted to go while pointing at our two loaded bikes. We haggled over the price and off we went.

Because I get motion sick, I sat up front with the driver. After small talk with the driver, I learned that he was only fourteen years old. With a big grin on his face, he told me that he would have his driver's license in a few more years. Even though he was young, he drove aggressively. After passing trucks on blind turns and generally disrespecting road safety, we arrived at the Pan American Highway. We were glad to have not been involved in a head-on collision or roll over. We were also away from another dangerous road and in the clear. We were back on the relatively safe Pan American Highway. We started climbing again and had a pleasant ride through the remainder of the Guatemalan Highlands. We camped in an unexciting spot in the tall grass satisfactorily out of sight of the road.

The next morning I got up early out of habit. I sat quietly, drinking coffee, and watching the day overcome the night. At times like this, the world is completely at peace. We were soon down the road again and enjoying the ride. For lunch, we found a truck stop and had the best lunch yet in Guatemala – I had Carne Adobado (meat marinated in a red chili sauce) and Cindie had chicken.

Trouble in Paradise

It was bound to happen. It happens to all touring cyclists eventually. I had to fix three flats that day, but that was just a hint of what was coming. I was riding along and suddenly I hit a small bump in the road. This much of a jolt is common, but it was the straw that broke the camel's back. My rear wheel had been giving me increasing trouble for weeks. I had trued it several times, but spokes still kept coming loose. This bump was the end of it. It knocked my wheel so out of true that it was not ridable. I laid the bike on its side and spun the rear wheel. It didn't get far before it hit the chain stays (frame) of the bike. I knew that my rim was in bad shape. I worked with my spoke wrench for a long time and finally got it rotating freely. I knew from experience that the wheel wouldn't last long like this. Luckily, there were no broken spokes. It was impossible to reattach my rear brakes, and I had to continue riding with only my front brakes.

It was after 4:00 p.m., and I was frustrated. We coasted slowly into Chimaltenango and asked two motorcycle cops where we could find a safe hotel. They escorted us to the only hotel that we saw in town. They told us that we would be safe there but not to wander around at night. In fact, this hotel shuts and locks the front doors shortly after sunset. Chimaltenango looked run down and had an above average number of drunks on the street. In the hotel, the owner had the same advice about not going out at night. When I asked him why, he told me that Chimaltenango was a notorious gathering place for hard-core drinkers and a large population of prostitutes.

During the night, we heard men laughing in the rowdy bars and giggling women trying to get their attention. In our room, we caught up on computer work and read our guidebooks. We learned that in the nearby village of San Andres Itzapa the cult of San Simon existed. It's said that

San Simon is the patron saint of the late night culture. San Simon is his Spanish name, Maximon is his Latino name and Ry Laj Man is his Mayan name. He is a combination of Mayan gods, Pedro de Alvarado (conquistador) and Judas.

The Cult of San Simon

In the morning, we decided we couldn't miss such a unique site. We took a taxicab to the San Simon shrine around 1 p.m.; many people visiting the shrine looked like they just had awakened. This crowd liked to hang around in late night bars. We waited in a line to take our turn at seeing the mannequin of San Simon. I was less interested in seeing his image than how the members of this cult paid their respects to him. San Simon was unlike any kind of saint that I had ever seen before. He looked like a high stakes player in a Las Vegas casino. He was actually a mannequin wearing a felt hat, modern suit and tie. In his hands were a bottle of rum and a big cigar. I am sure that the Pope doesn't approve of this place.

Haggard-looking women would chant thanks repeatedly and lay cash donations in San Simon's lap. Others would chant while unscrewing small bottles of cheap grain alcohol then they would drink it liberally and then slosh large amounts of the alcohol all over the saint in between drinks for themselves. Again, more cash, cigarettes and booze were laid in his lap. When it was our turn to come face to face with the saint of the late night crowd, I didn't know what to say. He certainly smelled like a drunk. I was astonished to see expensive half-full bottles of Johnny Walker and Jack Daniel's sitting around him. Then, I noticed a large wad of US greenbacks mixed in with local currency lying on is lap. Upon closer inspection, I noticed that several of the US bills were $10s and $20s. Wow, every definition of "loaded" was true for San Simon. We noticed that San Simon's face and hands were covered in plastic. It was obvious that this was necessary to protect his painted face and hands from the

San Simon.

corrosive effects of hard alcohol being continuously splashed on him. We finally gave him a quetzal (US$ .013), and I thanked him for the great time I'd had at Indiana University. We walked back through town and caught a bus back to our room.

Into Antigua

The next day I limped on into the city of Antigua on my bad wheel. The ride was pleasant because the weather was mild, and I tried to ignore the "thud thud" of my erratic wheel and the thought of it completely collapsing. This Sunday afternoon the local bike club was on this road in great numbers. I heard from several different concerned cyclists that my wheel looked bad or that my rear brakes weren't connected.

We stayed in Antigua for two weeks. Antigua is convenient and comfortable and not at all like the rest of Guatemala. We had heard from several other travelers what a great place it was. Our guidebooks called it the most beautiful colonial city in Central America. This was a welcome change, especially because we had bike repair work to do. Antigua had tons of tourists, modern-ish super markets, great internet access, McDonalds and many tour companies. Unfortunately it had its fair share of pushy hawkers. Antigua is a nice looking city with a glorious past, but reoccurring earthquakes turn old buildings into rubble here. In my opinion, it's not nearly as grand as the colonial silver towns of central Mexico like Zacatecas or Guanajuato nor as expensive.

Antigua had a large expatriate community that makes the bar and night life scene active. There is an Irish pub where we bought cans of Guinness beer and played trivia in English. Cindie and I both won a raffle and received free Gallo (Guatemala's most popular brand of beer) T-shirts as prizes. There are restaurants and cafes that specialize in showing English language movies. Cindie and I finally saw the movie Spider Man on Christmas day. For a small fee, we sat in a room with a dozen other people and watched a video. I am sure that this is a violation of international copyright laws, but nobody brought up the subject. Things are done differently in Latin America.

Antigua didn't have a modern bicycle shop, but Guatemala City, forty-five minutes away, did. We took a day trip into the city to buy a replacement rim and have it built on to my hub.

The trip into Guatemala City was a whole adventure packed into one day. We picked out a bike shop in the phone book and had a shuttle driver take us to the shop. This was expensive, but it made finding an address in the big city much easier. The first shop had moved, so the driver took us to another shop in the phone book at no extra charge. This high-end bicycle shop carried nothing but the best. The best rim they had in stock with thirty-six holes was a Mavic F519. We told the bike shop mechanic that we wanted to get the wheel built that same day. The rim cost US$40, the DT spokes cost US$15, and labor for building the wheel was US$10. It was obvious by the way the bicycle mechanic handled his tools that he was skilled and had built hundreds of wheels in his day.

We had a few hours to kill and decided to walk to the mall. We crossed a busy street in Guatemala City and into an upscale mall. Being in the mall during Christmas craziness reminded me of when I was a kid living near the mall in Greenwood, Indiana. This mall had three floors and sold mostly trendy name brands. It obviously catered to the affluent of the capital city, and everything was expensive. Everyone was friendly. We met three high school kids during their lunch break. They worked in a clothing store that sold Tommy and Polo Sport clothes. They went to expensive private bilingual schools and spoke fluent English. They even gave us free promotional T-shirts from their store. I was glad to see this side of Guatemala.

After the wheel was completed, we found a cheaper way back to Antigua. The problem was that it was already dark which made us nervous in a city with a bad reputation for crime. We caught a taxicab on the street to the bus station in downtown Guatemala City. This area looked extremely dangerous and crowded. As soon as we got out of the taxi-cab, a group of young men noticed us and immediately started walking in our direction. We were the only foreigners around and stuck out. I could be wrong, but my guess is that they were a ring of pickpockets. I have learned to trust my instincts while traveling. We quickly climbed into a retired American school bus bound for Antigua. The common name of this kind of public bus is the "chicken bus." It's called this because anything and everything including chickens can be found on board. During the cramped bus ride back to Antigua, Cindie and I played a game I called "what lane are we in." It was usually hard to tell and was surprising how many times the answer was "the middle lane" on a two-lane road.

We arrived in Antigua at 7:30 p.m. relieved to be back safe and unharmed. We walked down the deserted street back to our hotel room. In the end, I had a name brand rim built on my hub with quality spokes in a one day trip to the city.

Looking Down the Throat of a Smoking Volcano

I wanted to climb another active volcano and Cindie, being a Geologist, wanted to go without hesitation. Pacaya was the closest active volcano to Antigua. The guidebook says that Pacaya was a place where hikers were routinely robbed unless they hired a guide and armed guard and traveled with a large group of people. We paid 50 quetzals (US$6.60) for a full day tour. We met at 6:00 a.m. for the hour and a half drive to the base of Pacaya. At the park entrance, we paid another 25 quetzals (US$ 3.30) to enter.

The lower part of the hike was relatively easy. Once we climbed to the volcanic ridges and talus slope of Pacaya, the hike became extremely difficult. I climbed two steps up and slid one-step back all the way to the top. Cindie floated over

Pacaya.

Tim looking into the throat of Volcano Pacaya.

197

the cinders easier than I did; her ankle that she injured in Palenque didn't give her any trouble that day.

When we finally arrived at the top and reached the rim of the volcano, I could feel the temperature rise and smell toxic gases. Every now and then, the wind would change directions and blow the noxious gas on us and everybody would start coughing and moving away from the rim. While sitting on the rim eating our lunch, we could feel the ground grow hot and see it start to steam. Our group became alarmed, prepared to evacuate and then the ground would cool off again. I didn't have a good feeling looking down the throat of an active volcano that had erupted only five years earlier.

The best part of the whole hike was going straight down the side of the volcanic cone. Descending the talus slope was a lot like snow skiing. The cinders kept me floating on the top. The only thing that was missing was my poles. When we reached the bottom of the slope, we all had to sit down and remove the cinders from our shoes.

Christmas in Antigua

The Christmas holiday wasn't much different in Antigua from the USA. Familiar decorations were everywhere, including Santa, reindeer and even paper snowflakes in a place that never sees snow. The locals go through the same cycle as well. They shop, bake and prepare for family gatherings. Just like the rest of the Christian world, they don't get as much done as they expected and begin a mad rush as the deadline approaches. The day before Christmas, all the stores were having big sales and last minute shopping frenzy was happening everywhere. Credit cards were out and cash registers were singing that other Christmas song. People tried to be cheerful but looked tired and stressed out. Sound familiar?

La Merced, one of many churches in Antigua.

A big difference here was how fireworks played a major role in the celebrations. Makeshift stores were set up on the streets selling every type of amateur explosive imaginable at rock bottom prices. I could overhear the Mayan women in traditional dress, who always ran these stands, talking to the crowd. They were explaining to a group of eight-year-old boys what each brightly colored package with a fuse sticking out will do once lit. Nothing is illegal, and you can light them anywhere. It didn't matter if it was the crowded main

199

A little girl selling souvenirs.

plaza, busy sidewalk or in the street. Loud explosions were everywhere and all too common. When there was more or less a lull in traffic, little boys, who could barely strike a match, would rush to the middle of the street and set off terrifying rounds of firecrackers. We quickly learned to avoid groups of boys struggling with matches.

At one of the oldest and most famous churches in Antigua, La Merced, they were lighting the big fireworks, the same types used in professional displays in the USA. A nervous man was using his lit cigarette to ignite the big rockets, sending colorful explosions into the air. After they exploded in red and blue bursts, the burning remains fell on the crowd. I got lucky, but Cindie wasn't. A burning ember landed on her fleece jacket and burned a nasty hole. She wasn't alone; you could smell burning fabric and even hair all around us.

At the stroke of midnight on Christmas Eve, everyone

Santa in Antigua.

in town lit every explosive they had. The banging, popping and shaking went on for twenty minutes. Great clouds of smoke rose from the streets to engulf the city. It was what I pictured a war zone looking like except for the drunken guy in the Santa suit staggering around town.

After going into Guatemala City to get my rim replaced, it was obvious that there was no way to get Cindie to ride through that city's congestion. I didn't want to either. Some situations are worse than riding the bus. We needed to get to the other side of Guatemala City. The only first class bus (non chicken bus) that we could find going our way wouldn't stop until Rio Dulce several hours away. This was disappointing because the majority of the trip was downhill. We loaded our gear onto the bus in Antigua, changed buses in Guatemala City, and were on our way to Rio Dulce without incident.

We were glad we took the bus because at one of the stops, I noticed a strong headwind that would have blown us to a stop even on a downhill run, and it started raining hard. We arrived in Rio Dulce in the pouring tropical rain and quickly found a room. I gave each bike a quick check to see if it survived the cramped storage compartment under the bus. I always expect the worst, but everything checked out OK.

The day we arrived, it rained hard all night. We woke early and started packing for our side trip to the Mayan ruins of Tikal. Rio Dulce is a few meters above sea level and at this tropical latitude that means jungle. We were no longer in pine trees and crisp mountain air, but now it was January and not nearly as hot as our previous jungle experience in October in Tabasco and Palenque, Mexico.

First, we had to get to Flores, Guatemala. This would require another long bus ride up and back, but at least this time we were leaving our bikes behind in our hotel room. The bus is much more difficult in Guatemala compared to Mexico. It's also much cheaper. We had to haggle over the price of the tickets and then push and shove to secure a seat. That is when my nightmare began. The road to Flores had many turns, and I was feeling nauseous the entire way. I had to endure five hours of this while Cindie slept. She could do nothing, and there was no logic in making both of us suffer. We finally arrived about an hour before sunset, found a room, ate and went to bed early.

Tikal

Cindie herself best describes the famous Mayan ruins of Tikal. I believe that if she weren't a geologist she would have been an archeologist. Below is from Cindie's daily journal.

We woke at four a.m. to catch the five a.m. bus; we wanted to arrive at Tikal for sunrise at 6:15 a.m. We were in luck; the sky was clear, and the stars were out. It didn't look like *it was going to rain. A minivan finally picked us up at 5:20 a.m. Then they took us to a bus station: hey, we paid for a minivan to the ruins. It was the old "bait and switch and then wait" tactic commonly used on tourists. We waited on the bus until it filled with tourists. We left at 5:40 a.m. It was obvious by now that we weren't going to make sunrise at the ruins. We realized the bus from the 60's or 70's was a hunk of junk when it started moving. It could barely make it up the hills. I felt as if I could race up the hill with my bike faster. To slow things down even more, we were picking up people along the way. Then we had to stop and all pay for tickets at the entrance. I tried to use my student card from Spanish school in Mexico, but it didn't work. Foreigners pay 50 quetzals ($6.60) and nationals pay 15 quetzals ($2.0); Sundays are free for nationals. At least they get a break. I didn't mind paying more, but over three times more is too much.*

As soon as we got off the bus, Tim and I walked straight to the park entrance. We were trying to get some peace and quiet. It was a 15-minute walk through the jungle to the Grand Plaza. We walked through an area that hadn't been restored yet, and then we were behind Temple one. It rose dramatically 44 meters (144 feet) up out of the forest. We walked into the grand plaza where we were surrounded by restored Mayan temples. Temple 1 is the highest and steepest; no one can climb that Temple anymore. In the past, people have tumbled to their death on the steep stairs. Personally, I had no desire to climb up those steep and crumbling stairs. Temple 2 faces Temple 1 and has a superb view of the area as well. We meandered around the north acropolis and then set out for Temple 4. The jungle was alive with the noises of birds such as toucans and animals like the howler monkeys. Wild turkeys, tame turkeys would be more accurate, were strutting around showing off their multicolored feathers.

We met Melanie from the US at the top of Temple 4, and we decided to tour the ruins together. We first went to the

203

Temple 1, Mayan ruins of Tikal.

Lost World and climbed the pyramid close by. The sky was clear and the jungle was a dark shade of green; the air was heavy with humidity. Standing on the pyramid, we could see that three of the temples faced east, and one faced west. I wondered what the significance of this was. I read through the guidebook looking for the answer and didn't find one. Getting back down the pyramid was to be more of chore then going up. The stairs were large and steep.

We then went to the Seven Temples. The temples here in Tikal were huge, but they are also melting away in this environment. The Seven Temples were only visible where the trees have rooted themselves into the building. Everywhere else, the buildings are gone, physically dismantled by the tropical rain. We then took a side trail over to the Temple of Inscriptions and came across a group of howler monkeys. They sounded like a large gorilla twice their size. They were perched up in the top canopy of the jungle, a difficult place to get a good view of them.

We were all tired so we decided to stop at the restaurant for coffee. Just as we sat down the sky opened and the rain came down. The sun was out, yet it was raining hard. I thought this only happened in the deserts of Arizona – guess not.

After the rain, we tried to tour the rest of the ruins, but it had turned into a mud bog. We decided not to climb on any more pyramids; they looked more like slippery slides than ruins.

Down The Rio Dulce

Cindie and I agreed that the bus ride back to the town of Rio Dulce and our bikes was as miserable as the ride out. On this trip, the sly ticket collector on the bus tried to charge us double the fair price. I was tired of people trying to cheat us because we were foreigners in their country and perceived to be rich. Cindie refused to pay the inflated price of one hundred quetzals (US $13.40) per person in Spanish and loudly let him know she wasn't paying more than 50 quetzals (US $6.70) per person. When she was done with him, she paid him the fair price, and he never looked at us again. The other passengers on the bus, seeing how he tried to cheat us to fill his own pockets, gave him looks of disapproval. When we arrived back in the town of Rio Dulce we packed for the next day's boat trip down the River Rio Dulce.

In the morning, we took a short ride to the gas station to purchase gas for the stove. When I filled it up, it cost US$0.80 instead of the usual US$0.40. The price posted at the gas station was about the same as all of the others in Guatemala. I notified the attendant of the jump in price, and he nervously said, "I don't know." I was sure that I was being cheated. One clue was that when I had rolled up to the pump, where the attendant was and asked for gas, he had taken my fuel bottle and walked all the way across the station to a different pump. I now think that this was a special "Gringo Pump." Many tourists drive down from North America, especially Canada, or rent cars in Guatemala City. I didn't want to make a fuss over such a small amount of money, so I kept quiet and didn't tell Cindie about until later. She would have let him have it. Had I been in a car and seen my gas bill go from US$20 to US$40, I would have refused to pay it. This is an ugly form of discrimination that I wish wasn't part of traveling. Even though the vast majority of people we've done business with are fair and honest, a foreigner abroad sadly has to scrutinize all transactions.

We rode to the boat dock and worked at arranging a boat. The two loaded bikes gave the boat owners a lot of wiggle room in the negotiations. I bargained hard. I even walked away from a couple of guys because they took me for a fool. I finally found someone with a sense of reality and settled on a price. It had become clear lately how things work in countries that see corruption as a fact of life.

The boat ride down the river was fascinating because this area was nearly untouched by humans. Where people did live, it looked like they had a simple but pleasant life. Little kids in homemade boats swam and played in the water. They looked like they spent a good part of their young lives in the water. They were truly amphibious. Wildlife was everywhere including several colorful birds. The boat driver pulled up to a place where hot water bubbled out from the side of a limestone cliff.

Livingston

When we came ashore in Livingston we were greeted by friendly guys in dreadlocks that looked like they had spent twenty years at a Bob Marley concert. "Hay mon - welcome to par-a-deece mon - You be pedlin these bikes all around - SH#* mon - you be crazy, but I likes it a lots - your aces be a hurting for sure." This dialogue was great and never stopped. We pushed our bikes around looking for a room. We met everyone in town who wasn't out fishing.

Livingston is a unique place. It doesn't fit in with the rest of Guatemala. It has no roads to it, and the only way to get here is by boat. This cuts it off from the mainstream world and gives it a wild and lawless frontier feel. It's an unlikely place for a cycle tourist, but we wanted to experience it.

Livingston is at the crossroads of three countries. Frequent ferries run from here to Belize, Honduras and Puerto Barrios, Guatemala. So it's border town. More notable is that Livingston is a mixture of several different cultures or ethnic groups. Everyone speaks two or more languages. There are Gruifuna (Black Carib) who speak English (Belizean) and Spanish, indigenous Mayan who speak Quiche and Span-

A house along the Rio Dulce river.

207

Marco showed us where the available rooms were in Livingston.

Tapado, seafood soup with coconut milk and banana.

Long time resident of Livingston.

ish, and Latinos who speak Spanish and one of the other languages. It's an incredibly funky town to say the least; everyone gets along well, and for a small place, there is a great variety of food, music and traditions.

Because Livingston is a sea town, it had sailors who see the world on their private sailboats. These "Popeye" looking people who have been at sea for a long time made the most of their time in port. They were a scruffy bunch with the sea in their veins and wild stories of surviving storms and exotic distant lands. We could always spot them because of their head-to-toe tans, torn up cutoffs and expensive raincoats. They were also buying supplies by the wheelbarrow load. Their sailboats were sophisticated, like floating RVs but much more self-sufficient. They have solar panels, water desalination equipment, wind generators and all manner of communication and navigation equipment. They could go all over the world free as the wind. If only I didn't get seasick.

We stayed a week in Livingston, including New Year's Eve, and saw something different every day. One of the things that will forever stick in my mind is that people from such diverse races, religions and cultures can live together in peace. This is a shining example of how the world should be. I would like to take the leaders from the nations with race and religion conflicts (you know which ones they are) and bring them here on a field trip. I would say, "Look everyone is different. They go to different kinds of churches and have different colors of skin. Do you see how no one wants to fight a war because of these differences? Peace - It can be done. Your wars will never bring a solution to your problems. They never have. Your only solution is to figure out what comes so easily to the people of Livingston, Guatemala."

Puerto Barrios

From Livingston we rode another boat back to the mainland and the city of Puerto Barrios. Puerto Barrios is a rough port town. It's the only place where goods carried by boat come in and out of Guatemala on the Caribbean side. Truckloads of bananas, coffee and pineapples fill the boats while TVs, cars and other manufactured goods are unloaded. Many merchant marines who have spent months at sea drink themselves into oblivion when they get to a port town like this. Throw in hundreds of truckers who drive the goods all over the country with the same night-life ambitions, and a seedy place like Puerto Barrios develops. The bars or cathouses weren't good places to walk nearby at night. To make things worse, everything was dirty: backed-up, open, smelly and disgusting sewers everywhere. I have come to accept that many countries dump their sewage in the ocean, but to have giant open pools of it on the sides of the streets is plain nasty.

On the ferry to Puerto Barrios, our bikes had the best seat.

Church at San Andreas Xecul.

Indigenous woman at San Andreas Xecul.

11 Honduras: So Much Poverty

(January 7 - 31, 2003)

The day that we crossed from Guatemala into Honduras was crazy and at times scary. As we were packing to leave Puerto Barrios, Cindie found a large amount of Guatemalan quetzales in her panniers. We were stashing money in several different places because we had been so concerned about being robbed in Guatemala. This currency would be worthless in Honduras, and we weren't sure that we could exchange Guatemalan quetzals for Honduran lempiras at the small border town. We loaded our bikes and rode to the bank to exchange the quetzales to US dollars. This took forty-five minutes because of the long line at the bank. We think that we lost about US$5 in the exchange, but at least we had more greenbacks to add to our emergency cash fund of US $300 cash that we stored in Cindie's rear pannier. The US dollar is easily exchanged in Central America, and we like to keep a decent quantity of small bills around for emergencies, such as the bank being closed or our ATM card not working.

When Cindie emerged from the bank, we were ready to hit the road. We anticipated this would be a long day because we had a border to cross. As I climbed on my bike, I discovered that my front tire was flat. This was the fifth one in a row, and this time I was determined to find the cause. Sure enough, I found a tiny piece of glass hiding in the tread of the tire. I pried it out, changed the tube, and we were finally off to another country.

The terrain was flat because we were crossing a large tropical river delta that separates Guatemala and Honduras. We were riding among huge banana plantations or "fincas" as they are called here. They stretched as far as the eye could

Tim changing his fifth flat in a row.

see. The friendly workers greeted us while on their lunch breaks. We would wave first, and 150 men would wave back. Life on the finca looked like hard work, but the people had shelter, food and clothing.

Fear From Above

While happily riding among the banana fields towards the border of Honduras, in the distance we saw a yellow airplane flying low and spraying something on the bananas. I knew the exact moment that the pilot saw us. The small plane immediately climbed and then dove towards us. At first, I thought the pilot wanted to get a closer look at the two strange cyclists and maybe show off. Boy, was I ever wrong. The plane flew just above the bananas on a course that intersected ours. It was close enough to see that the pilot was wearing a New York Yankees baseball cap. The pilot turned on the sprayer and a thick blanket of red slime

214

was neatly laid down on us. It was terrible. We had nowhere to hide and knew that whatever was coming out of that plane was some sort of toxic pesticide. I assumed that this chemical was banned in the USA for years. The red gel was everywhere: it covered my arms and legs, and I inhaled a fair amount as well. Was this an accident? Why would someone do such a thing?

My first question was quickly answered. The plane circled around and came in low. It was obvious that he was going to spray us again. We picked up our pace in a futile attempt to out run the flying terrorist. The plane had to correct its course a little to compensate for our increased speed, but he sprayed us thoroughly. I felt like we were storming the beach and being strafed by a WWII fighter. Our only hope was to get to the Honduran border. My thinking was that the airplane couldn't cross the international border. The pilot sprayed us one more time before we arrived at the border. As we neared the gate, the plane disappeared. We were glad to see him go and still bewildered as to why he had sprayed us.

The Line in the Mud

The Honduran border was almost painless. We received our exit stamps and paid our exit fee (10 quetzales or US$1.30/person) to leave Guatemala. The border guard didn't ask us any of the usual questions about guns or drugs. He was completely uninterested in what was in our bags. When I told him about the crop duster purposely spraying us he thought it was funny. It was obvious that he wasn't going to doing anything about it. He directed us to the immigration office to get our entry stamps. We had to pay twenty Honduran lempiras or US$1.30/person entry fee. After paying our entry fee, we went to the nearest bathroom, one that wasn't very clean, and washed the residue of the red slime off.

Cindie crossing the border from Guatemala to Honduras.

We decided to eat in the small border town since it would be another fifty kilometers (thirty-one miles) before our next stop. At a small restaurant next to the immigration office, we parked our bikes and sat in the outdoor eating area. While I was ordering our food, I had my back to Cindie and our two loaded bikes. In the corner of my eye, I noticed two teenage boys looking at our bikes. This was common because kids are normally interested in bicycles. When I turned to ask Cindie what she wanted to drink, I saw quick movements near our bikes. Something was up.

We didn't keep anything valuable in our outside pockets of our bike bags. Buried deep in Cindie's bags were all our important items. We kept a daily amount of money and our camera in my handlebar bag. This was the only vulnerable area, and I could see my handlebar bag sitting safely in front of Cindie with her hand on it. Still, red flags were going up for me.

216

I shot the boy my look that conveyed, "You're busted – get away from my bike." He didn't move. I finished ordering with my back to the counter woman and my eyes on our bikes and the boy's hands. The kid, seeing that I was watching, finally moved on. Later, after we started riding, I noticed Cindie's seat bag was unzipped. We stopped and found that everything was there. I am now convinced that this was the cause of the sudden movement from the boy. If he had been quicker, he would have gotten an inner tube and a couple of plastic tire levers. We were learning to watch our belongings closer at border crossings.

Twenty kilometers Down A Mud Road

The next obstacle was a twenty kilometer (12.5 miles) muddy road. Everyone from money changers to border guards had been warning us about this road. The general advice was, don't attempt this road if it's raining because it can become impassable to all but 4x4 trucks. It hadn't rained for several hours, and there had even been the occasional moment of sun to dry things out. We could see mud covered trucks, American school buses and even low-clearance passenger cars coming towards us. We thought that if they could make it so could we. This was as good of a chance as there had been in several days because of the regular showers.

As we started down the mud road and into a new country, we found it manageable. The road had standing water and was messy, but our tires only sank in so far before they found something solid enough to roll on. It was a lot of work to plow through the muck, and our progress was slowed to crawl. I could see that our bikes, bags, clothes and our bodies were going to need a good cleaning after this. We inched along but had the jungle and the occasional banana plantation to look at. We stopped and took a few pictures of the surroundings. The excitement of a new country – currency, accent and unforeseen Honduran adventures – was swirling around

217

in our heads. After all, we had already had toxic pesticides sprayed on us and an attempted robbery. What else could happen? Surely, we had reached our quota for the day.

Then it started to rain. It went from partly cloudy to rain in a matter of minutes. This wasn't a light rain but instead was the heavy tropical variety that comes straight down and instantly soaks everything. Our road, that was difficult before, turned to a river of mud. When I thought the rain had reached peak intensity, it pounded even harder. We pulled over to put on our raincoats and assess the situation. At least the rain had washed off the rest of the pesticides sprayed on us earlier. I was learning that a raincoat in this kind of rain isn't meant to keep you dry. Nothing could do that. A raincoat in this situation is more like a wet suit that keeps you warm while under water. We also removed our helmets and put on our baseball caps with a bill. This kept the rain a few inches from our eyes so vision was possible.

Our situation was bad. We had at least ten more kilometers (6.3 miles) of the mud road and thirty more kilometers (18.8 miles) of pavement before we could find lodging. We were in the middle of nowhere and not sure how much longer the road conditions would allow us to continue. Everything around us looked wet and uninviting. I supposed that if I'd had more experience in the jungle, we would have camped somewhere. We decided that our best option was to keep going and try to reach the pavement before we had to push the bikes. At least everything in our waterproof bags was dry.

I was less concerned about the road when a bus motored by. I said, "If that old thing can make it, then we can, too." We had no other choice. We were able to pedal our machines. My front rim was completely submerged below the mud. It was so deep at times that my foot actually went into the mud on the bottom of every revolution of the cranks. I looked

218

at my drive train, but all that I could see was mud clumps with a chain running through it. Fortunately, we both had shifted to our lowest gear over an hour before and hadn't tried to shift since. Cindie's head was down, and she looked like she was on a death march. She said nothing. I tried to make light of our situation and cheer Cindie up. I yelled over the pounding rain. "We should bottle this mud and sell it as bike oil. I think that it works better than oil." She didn't even look up. Not once, even in our hardest of times, had she even mentioned giving up. I decided to leave her alone and let her deal with this in her own way. We caught up with a floundering overloaded banana truck as the rain started to slack off. We followed for a while before we had breathed in enough exhaust and passed it in a straight section.

The rain finally stopped all together. We started to see more traffic. Cindie pointed out that the trucks coming towards us were appearing less and less dirty. We took this

The truck full of bananas that we eventually passed.

as a sign that they hadn't been on the muddy road as long. Good news can be found in the strangest places on days like these. I could see a truck stopped ahead; the driver was out examining the road condition. He was obviously trying to decide if the road was passable or not. As we passed him, he stared at us and studied the state of our bikes. I am sure that we looked bad, I wish that I had taken a picture of us. I seriously thought about it, but the camera was dry and clean where it was and I didn't want to change that. On the other side of that truck was the pavement.

It was getting dark, and we still had thirty kilometers (18.8 miles) to go. We wrestled our bikes into a big gear (the mud on our cassettes prevented us from changing gears) and started cruising on the flat pavement. Cindie slipped into my draft, and I worked at keeping us above twenty-five kph (sixteen mph). The setting sun actually poked through the clouds, and I saw our shadows riding beside us down the road. Soon we had the ocean on our left and jungle-covered mountains on our right. We stopped at a gas station to get something to drink. The mud had made our water bottles unusable, and I was starting to feel dehydrated. A Gruifuna man, who spoke a form of English, insisted that he pour buckets of water on our rigs. He actually made a big improvement in our drive trains (cassette, chain and crank). He wanted nothing in return and wished us luck on the rest of our journey. The remainder of the ride into Omoa went smoothly. I felt like we had earned it. We rolled in after dark with our flashing red taillights on, pitched our tent in a campground, enjoyed a hot shower and went to bed.

The Beach at Last

Omoa, Honduras was our first real ocean beach. We had been traveling for over nine months and somehow had avoided the beach. We had seen several pictures of Omoa in a Guatemalan newspaper. It looked like a perfect Carib-

Tim and Cindie at the beach in Omoa.

bean beach paradise. Maybe it was, but all we saw was rain, drizzle, fog, clouds and more rain. All the locals said that this was supposed to be the dry season. To make things even more interesting, the only place we could afford to stay was the camping area at a traveler's hostel. The only creatures that didn't seem to mind the rain were the abundant mosquitoes. They thought it was feast time. I am starting to believe that mosquitoes crave Chloroquine, the anti-malaria drug that we take when we are in these tropical zones.

We did go to the beach. It was dark and cloudy of course. I can now say that I went to the beach with no sun block and had to wear a raincoat. We took a couple of open kayaks out for a spin. It rained the whole time. I would be lying if I didn't admit that the rain took the romance out of our boat outing.

It wasn't all bad. The hostel had a kitchen and a common sitting area under a roof. There we met people from all over the world. We were the only Americans, as usual, and because of this, we were asked questions. I learned a great deal about European politics. We talked late into the night. Everyone was as blue as I was because of the constant rain. Most of the others had big plans to go to the bay islands. These islands are famous for SCUBA diving on the world's second largest coral reef. After they read the weather report on the internet – ten more days of rain – everyone changed plans. Most were taking a bus to the Pacific side of the country and better weather. We also looked at the weather, which was better inland and even sunny at the other end of this small country. We had plans for leaving town the next day as well. Rain or shine.

On our final wet evening, everyone gathered around the table for a celebration. I saw movement under the table and thought that it was a rat. I told the group, and everyone jumped out of their seats and pulled out flashlights. It was a large crab. Apparently, it was the same type that's served in restaurants because it was dropped into a pot of boiling water. The crab must have been good because even the people initially opposed to killing it wanted a taste. I am not much for seafood, so I didn't have any. Cindie said that it was good.

Seat Binder Bolt

The morning of our departure was clear. We packed things up damp and hit the road. We rode fast and hard on the flat road and made good time. Twenty kilometers (12.5 miles) out of Omoa, on the outskirts of Puerto Cortez, I noticed that my seat position felt low. I assumed that all the wet weather had caused the seat post to slip into the frame. We stopped and I pulled out my Allen key set and raised the seat about a centimeter (0.4 inches). As I was tightening the binder bolt, it broke in half. Without this bolt, the seat slid down to the frame. With my seat position so low, I was unable to do any serious riding. This broken little piece of metal rendered my whole bicycle practically useless. I said to Cindie, "Well, it looks like another test of our resourcefulness." Cindie wasn't amused; she lost her patience with the situation and was visibly upset.

People in Honduras, typical of Latin Americans, routinely used bicycles as transportation. Anytime we had been in or near a city, there had been hordes of bicycles buzzing around. I closely examined people as they rode by to see how their seat posts, were held up. Many of the mountain bikes had what I needed. One friendly guy stopped and asked me in his heavy Honduran Spanish what I was looking for. I pointed at his binder bolt and then showed him my broken one. He immediately understood and told us to follow him to a bike shop. We stopped at a place that I would have never guessed was a bike shop and he asked the owner for a binder bolt. Even though I could see a few basic parts, inner tubes, chickens, turkeys and the usual pack of stray dogs, the owner didn't have a binder bolt. The three of us peddled off to two more "bike shops"; still we couldn't find a binder bolt.

As we were riding along, I looked at his bike and noticed that he not only had the part that I wanted, but he had a fancy (for Honduras) quick release. It was now 1:00 p.m., and we still had 67 kilometers (42 miles) to go to get to Honduras' second largest city, San Pedro Sula.

This city had a bad reputation for crime, and we definitely wanted to be in a hotel room before dark. I offered him some lempiras to buy his binder bolt. I don't think that he totally understood me. I pulled out a fifty lempira note (approximately US$3) and motioned that we make an exchange. This must have been a lot of money for this part because he had it off his bike and on mine before I knew it. I didn't mind over paying him because he had been willing to ride all over town to help us out and never even suggested that we pay for his help.

I adjusted my seat and down the road we went. I still have this binder bolt to this day.

As soon as we turned south, we caught a wonderful tailwind and flew on our last stretch of flat road in Honduras. It took us three hours to reach San Pedro Sula, and it didn't even rain on us the entire day. It was cloudy, but that kept the tropical sun at bay.

San Pedro Sula

When we arrived in San Pedro Sula, we had an hour of daylight left. This is usually plenty of time to find a room. Our routine is to first find the central plaza, then locate a place for me to sit and watch the bikes and talk to locals while Cindie looks around with our guidebooks and comparison shops for a room. As soon as we found a place to sit in the plaza, a police officer came walking up. Surprisingly, he spoke good English. He told us that bikes weren't allowed in the plaza. I promised him that we wouldn't ride them. He told me that bicycles weren't allowed to be parked there either. He told me, "We are trying to make our city look modern." I have learned a long time ago not to argue with a Latin American official, and we were back on the busy street. I wondered if city officials thought that no modern city was complete without air pollution. Stray hungry dogs running around are OK, but bicycles aren't. I will never understand why they chose to chase cyclists away from the city park and not dogs.

Now, the problem was that we had to push our bikes around a large unknown city and look for a room. This exposed us to pickpockets and other slimy types. We took the first room that looked reasonable and safe. It was more expensive than we would have liked, but it had an endless hot shower. We stayed in San Pedro Sula for several days and enjoyed several hot showers as opposed to the cold showers we had grown accustomed to lately.

From San Pedro Sula it was flat, and then we had a long (forty kilometers, twenty-five miles) uphill ride before the next town. It had been cloudy and drizzly all day. It looked like it was about to rain hard. We knew that we would never make it to a town with a hotel before dark. We pulled off the road to discuss our options. We didn't have any good ones. This is the downside of our carefree lack of travel plans. We don't always know where we are going to stay. Suitable ground for camping in the jungle was hard to find. Everything was soggy and full of mosquitoes. We had been in this fix dozens of times before and had learned not to panic. We concluded that something would turn up. As we were standing there trying to determine our location on the map, a man appeared from a group of buildings across the street. He introduced himself as Marco and asked us if we needed something. He spoke English in a familiar North American accent. We told him of our lack of safe lodging. I noticed that the sign on the gate announced that the property was part of the Christian Church. He told us that we should come into the compound and meet his father who ran the place. His name was Bob, and he explained that the compound was a minister training school for the church. He and Marco were in the process of getting ready for opening day.

They were American and had family near our hometown of Prescott, Arizona. We were further surprised to learn that they had connections in Greenwood and Mooresville, Indiana. I had grown up in Greenwood and my brother lives in Mooresville. We laughed at what a small world it is. I asked if we could camp behind one of their buildings out of sight of the road. Being hidden was always a priority when camping in that part of the world. Bob would have nothing of it and invited us to stay in the future residence house. As we were walking over to the house, he repeatedly apologized

225

for the condition of the house. He explained that they were still working on it.

When we went inside, it was much nicer than Bob had led us to believe. Yes, it was under construction, but it had a bathroom complete with a toilet seat, an electrical outlet to charge the computer and even a bed to sleep in. Bob had no reason to apologize to us. Cindie and I couldn't believe our luck. We happened to stop in front of the right place. That evening, before they went home, we all sat and talked. Bob and Marco answered our many questions about Honduras. Bob told us that Honduras suffered terribly from the 1998 hurricane Mitch. Hurricane Mitch was so powerful that they had found farmers' bodies that were washed down rivers hundreds of kilometers from their homes. People's houses, farms and business had been literally wiped from the earth. The scars of that natural disaster were sadly easy to see. We couldn't help but feel sorry for people. I don't believe that regular working people have insurance in Honduras and many had to start completely over. Temporary houses, made out of pieces of wood, cardboard, and scrap metal were put up everywhere.

Bob and Marco also told us of a side road to get to our next destination, Lake Yojoa. We were happy to learn of a different road with less traffic and more scenery. It rained that night as we slept, but we were happily indoors.

Up Into the Mountains

The next day we got an early start. We quickly found the road that our new American friends had described. This was a great road for cycling. It had little traffic and we saw the day-to-day life for the majority of Hondurans. We rode past large sugar cane fields and pineapple farms. It was sugar cane harvest time and men were busy in the fields with pack animals of every description loaded down with the sugar cane. It was a glimpse into yet another world. We were off the beaten track.

We climbed and climbed through exotic and interesting villages. People are friendly in rural Honduras, and we often stopped and talked. The friendly Hondurans will talk your ear off. There was much to learn from them, for they truly saw things differently. This is the advantage to bicycle travel: we had much more human contact compared with

Tim eating sugar cane.

227

those on the bus. One of the disadvantages is that we have to eat constantly. We stopped at a large waterfall for lunch.

After lunch, we climbed through a gentle rain until we reached Lake Yojoa. This is probably a scenic lake. I say probably because we never saw the lake: we only saw rain and clouds. We took a long break at a viewpoint and soaked in the quietness. We pushed on to the turn off to a remote National Park that we wanted to visit. We saw a sign that announced the park as seven kilometers (4.4 miles) away. Seven kilometers isn't much, but the dirt road was a mud bog because of the past few weeks of foul weather. The last time we rode on such a road, we'd had to spend days cleaning everything. This was supposed to be the dry season, but the weather was behaving more like the rainy season. We opted for a ride in a pickup truck. We easily found a truck and negotiated a price. It was a good thing we were in the truck because the road was steep in places and we lost traction and slid often even though we were in four-wheel drive.

Parque National Cerro Azul Meambar

The Parque National Cerro Azul Meambar is a misty cloud forest and incredibly wet. It's a cloud forest because of its altitude and unique location. It was raining everywhere else in Honduras anyway, so a place that was supposed to be cloudy and rainy was perfect. At least we didn't feel cheated by the weather. All of the plant life competed for the scant amount of light. Cindie noticed several of the plants were the same as common houseplants sold in the USA. This park is known for its animal and especially bird inhabitants. We saw a wide variety of exotic birds making every kind of sound imaginable. One of them sounds like a cell phone ringing. We also heard Toucans in the trees, but we never saw them.

For three days, we were the only visitors to this special place. We hung out with the caretaker but had difficulty with his thick Honduran accent. We spent one whole day on a

Cindie on our hike through the cloud forest.

long hike that took us high into the cloud forest. It may have been my imagination, but the dense lush plant life made the air supercharged with oxygen. We had a lot of energy.

Running On Empty

The day we left the park was yet another wet, overcast and drizzly day. At this point, we had been dealing with four weeks of damp rainy weather. I even lost the biker tan lines from the gloves and long shorts. Nothing was completely dry. Both of our bikes were constantly covered in road grime and mud. Rust was invading everything metal. All of our gear that was shiny new ten months ago now looked worn and tattered.

The months on the move were also starting to catch up with me. We both looked up at the angry sky that was surely going to dump on us before this day was over. I thought that at least riding would warm me up from the chill that I couldn't shake. We rode maybe a kilometer down the road when a long line of makeshift shanty houses appeared by the road. Dirty kids were running around barefoot or sitting in a deep depression staring off into space. These houses were made from tin, cardboard boxes and scrap wood. There was no running water, electricity or even a door on the houses. These people were desperately poor and struggling so hard to hold on, were probably victims of Hurricane Mitch, but I had no way to know without asking. I wanted to ride fast and think about it later. A coward's way out, but I could think of nothing else to do. We were helpless to improve their situation; there were too many people to help. Living without the basic necessities of life shouldn't be reality for anyone.

The sewer was an open ditch that stunk along the road. There was no source of clean water. They also were dealing with the weather. They had no way to escape. They had no bicycle to ride off on nor ATM card to get more cash when they needed it. The hardest thing to try to block out was the dozens of kids that would yell out to us in sincere desperation, "Gringo, Gringo una lempira (US$0.06)" or beg for food with "Tengo hombre (I am hungry)." It was more than I was ready to cope with in my already-tired mind.

As I was looking at all of this injustice, I guess that I wasn't watching the road. I rolled over a large piece of glass that loudly sliced through my front tire. I found myself standing on the side of the road looking at a large cut in my tire. We weren't going anywhere fast. Off came my panniers. I used the old bicycle rider's trick of finding something to put behind the cut to keep the tube from coming through the hole in the tire. This is called a "boot" in biker lingo and all cyclists have done it at one time or another. I needed to figure out what to use for my boot. Back home I would have used a green US one dollar bill. Money works well because it's stronger than average paper. Here in Honduras I would have to settle for local currency. At least here, I could fix seventeen tires with one lempira bills for the cost of one US dollar. The problem was how to pull out money around such poverty.

By this time, we had drawn a good size crowd of bored kids. As they gathered around, we could see that about half of them were suffering from disease. We saw countless oozing sores, eyes swollen shut and constant scratching. Two young girls were standing nearby; one was holding a baby, and the baby had numerous bedbug bites on its face. These kids were in bad shape. If I could, I would have hired a bus and taken the whole lot to a hospital.

Cindie kept my handle bar bag closed while she stuck her hands in and fumbled with the wallet. She found the one lempira note and handed it to me. Every kid in sight saw this and wondered what was next. When they saw me cram it between my tire and tube, they were shocked. To them it must have been the same as someone burning US twenty dollar bills to keep warm. I put everything back together and was glad that my boot worked. This was by far the most difficult flat to fix ever. In the future, "When I have to fix a flat, let it be in the worst traffic or even on a busy bridge. Let it rain or snow on me, but never again do I want to stand around with all of my money and toys in front of such hopeless kids." I will never look at the world the same after this experience. I will see a world where the basic needs of life aren't always attainable. This is something I assumed everyone had until I ventured away from home.

The rest of the day, we spent slowly riding up a mountain for five hours. This gave us time to reflect on the ordeal of changing the flat, and too much time to remember the smells and misery of that shantytown.

I have no solutions to this problem of extreme poverty. I am starting to see that it exists in all parts of the world. It probably always has. The best I can do is let the world know such conditions exist. As you read this in your comfortable office or home, please remember that those kids are still out there somewhere wishing for a fraction of what most of us consider the necessities of life.

On To the Capital

That night we stopped in a roadside hotel that usually caters to truck drivers and traveling salesmen. We were wet and cold. I ran our stove in the room for hours to warm our room and dry our clothes. We burned almost an entire liter (0.26 gallons) of gasoline. Cindie made us hot soup, and we dreamed of the dry Arizona desert.

The next morning we saw the sun. As soon as it came through our window, we had all of our clothes and equipment out to dry. After weeks of everything being damp, finally we were dry. We had a celebration with coffee and oatmeal. We had finally ridden far enough into the interior of Honduras to escape the rain. This marked a permanent change in the weather. From now on, it was half sun and half clouds, but at least it seldom rained. I felt we had passed another test of our will to continue.

We rode on several days towards the capital. We stopped for a few days in the city of Comayagua for a much-needed rest. This was another town that didn't allow bikes in their main plaza. Again, a police officer ran us off.

We rode through scenic mountains until we were finally on a high point looking down into the large city of Tegucigalpa, Honduras' capital. We descended into heavy traffic at blazing speeds. We had to dodge burro trains loaded with coffee, broken glass in the street and city buses that couldn't decide on the correct lane. We stopped and asked a group of taxi drivers to show us where we were on our map and how to get to the main plaza. None of them agreed on anything. They were entertaining. A friendly and respectful debate broke out concerning our questions. I thought that taxi

Camping in Honduras.

drivers would know the city better. We miraculously forgot all of our Spanish and claimed that we didn't understand them. We got away. Those guys are probably still debating the way to the plaza to this day.

We caught up with an old man on a one-speed bike and asked him directions. He told us to follow him. He was fearless in traffic. We found ourselves on interstate-like on-ramps and four-lane roads. He reached his destination and pointed down a road on which we were supposed to continue. After several more map checks we finally found the center of town and the cheap hotels.

Tegucigalpa wasn't what we expected. Because it's the capital and largest city in Honduras, we thought it would be a dirty and dangerous place. Neither of our guidebooks painted the best picture either. Once we were in the historic center, however, we found it to be pleasant and safe during the day. We didn't run around in any big city at night. There

233

is interesting architecture, and several of the roads were permanently closed off to cars and turned into pedestrian-only areas.

We visited the old church and attractive plaza. Most of the inhabitants were prosperous and friendly. We saw many Asian people, and businesses, and restaurants catered to them. This diversity isn't common in Latin America and was refreshing. We ate chow mien noodles, Kung Pao chicken and fried rice once a day. I don't know the story about how the Asians immigrated to Honduras, but I'll bet it's a good one.

Our hotel was near all of the international embassies including the American embassy. I had never been in an embassy before, so we decided to make a visit. The US embassy was large and looked like a fortress. We went in and were surprised at the services offered. We found all of the tax forms and learned that there is even specific tax information and procedures for Americans living abroad. Can you believe that the tax man can stick his hands in your pockets all the way down here? It proves that you can run, but you cannot hide.

We saw the French, German, Austrian, Mexican and Canadian embassies and many more. It was an upscale and international part of town. We saw high-ranking government officials cruising around in their luxury sedans with bulletproof glass. Cindie found a grocery store that catered to this crowd. Most grocery stores in Central America have a limited selection. We considered ourselves lucky if we could find peanut butter; usually they have the basics such eggs, beans, sugar and vegetable oil. This store had so many choices we suffered culture shock. They even took Visa at the checkout line. All these choices came at a price. They sold boxes of chocolate Pop Tarts at $4.50 per box: we passed. I was tempted. Cindie went hog-wild. I had to put things back because the cart was so full. I had to stop her

Cindie leaving Tegucigalpa.

before it was necessary to buy a burro to carry it all back to the hotel. I never saw anyone get so much pleasure out of a grocery store. On the walk back to the hotel, I had six bags in each hand. I also knew somehow this all had to fit on my bicycle. We found, among other things, a large jar of peanut butter, jelly, brown rice, Pringles Potato Chips and a can of Hormel chili.

The Road to the Nicaraguan Border

The road to the Nicaraguan border was a mountainous journey that consisted of three days riding and two nights in the tent. At first, the climb out of Tegucigalpa was steep and went through an extremely poor area. Once we were out of the urban area, we ascended into a healthy pine forest. In mid-afternoon, it started to rain, so we set up camp high in the mountains with beautiful views of the sweeping valleys below. We stayed up and listened to the Voice of America

Cindie riding in Honduras.

(VOA) news on our shortwave radio as we gazed at the blanket of stars above. That night, Cindie kept waking me up to tell me she heard something outside. I would crawl out of the tent with a flashlight and poke around until I was satisfied that nothing was out there. As I lay there awake listening to the still of the night and Cindie snore, she woke with a start and told me she heard voices outside of the tent. Since I was already awake and hadn't heard anything, I knew she was having a bad dream. Needless to say, neither one of us slept well that night.

The second night we had to push our bikes through tall grass to find a hidden place to camp. I newly learned that

236

Cindie had a fear of tall grass. She said that she always thinks that she is going to step on a snake. I took her picture to attempt to take her mind off the task. We found a suitable spot behind a hill and had a peaceful night.

On our last ride in Honduras, we descended into tobacco growing country and the sweet smell of tobacco. We rode past factories where dozens of old women were hand-rolling cigars. I could remember seeing Honduran cigars in fancy smoke shops, and now I have an image of someone's grandmother rolling huge stogies.

Ladies rolling cigars.

Camping in Honduras.

Tim crossing the border from Honduras to Nicaragua.

12 Nicaragua: Sandinistas and Contras

(February 1 – 20, 2003)

Crossing the border from Honduras to Nicaragua was much different from the previous borders. The big excitement was the red tape involved in getting our bikes out of Honduras. To leave Honduras the exit guards wanted to see a registration or proof of ownership for our bikes. I'm not exactly sure what they wanted because all they kept asking for was a "documento" or document. As they were insisting that we provide them with our bike papers, I was sure that they knew we didn't have any. I believe they have worked this scam on other cyclists before. I gave them one of our flyers in an attempt to change the subject. They weren't interested. We were again asked for our bike papers. They said that we were supposed to get the bike papers when we entered Honduras. No such thing existed at that border crossing. I learned that we wouldn't receive our exit stamps without this paperwork. Without exit stamps we wouldn't be allowed into Nicaragua.

The whole thing sounded fishy to me. They were poor actors, but pretended to be disturbed at our lack of papers for our bikes. I knew that I was going to have to bribe my first Latin American official. I said to the border official in Spanish "Can I pay you the official fee now and have you straighten out the paperwork for me later?"

He mentioned a sum of Honduran lempiras that I roughly calculated to equal US$25.

I laid a crisp green US$5 dollar bill on the table and apologized for not having local currency. It was my turn to lie. I did this in hopes that he couldn't calculate the value quickly. People in Latin America like to save money in US currency.

He smiled and said that he would have to buy stamps, paper and envelopes. He wanted more.

I pulled out another US$5 dollar bill and told him if it cost more that I would have to go to a Honduran bank and cross the border somewhere else. I even pulled out my map and pointed at a different border crossing. He knew that I had more cash on me. He complained about the high cost of stamps. I grabbed the ten dollars from the table and started to leave. I turned my voice from cheerful to stern. I said that I had no more money and would have to cross somewhere else. He quickly called me back and said that he could arrange the paperwork for me for US$10 dollars. He stamped our passports, and we were gone. We didn't shake hands, and I never received a receipt for my payment.

We pushed our bikes one hundred meters (328 feet) to the Nicaraguan immigration office. Cindie went in to get our entry stamps. I wanted to stay with the bikes because I noticed an ice cream vender motion to a group of boys to look in our direction.

As the boys approached I noticed a large poster proudly stating that Nicaragua doesn't allow bribes and to report any attempts of bribery to a special office in Managua. It even gave a phone number to call if you had trouble. All of the entry and exit fees were clearly displayed on the wall. I read that it was going to cost forty cordobas (US$3, each) entrance fee and another sixty cordobas (US$4 each) to buy a tourist card. I could probably have gotten by cheaper with a bribe system. All this was straight forward enough, but Cindie reported that the official wanted us to fill out a vehicle form for each bike. She had to go into a different office to start this process.

By then young boys surrounded me. They asked numerous questions. I laid my bike on its side, grabbed my handle bar bag, (with our camera), and stepped back so I could easily see both bikes. The boys tried to talk to me. They asked me where I was from and how much the bikes cost. I answered that I don't understand any Spanish in hopes that they would leave. They tried other ways to get my attention away from the bikes, but I wouldn't turn my head. One of the boys even acted like he fell and hurt himself and another asked if I had a bandage, I still refused to turn my head or understand what they were saying.

They kept edging closer to the bikes until finally one of them started running his hands on my rear panniers. He was testing me to see how far he could go. I forcefully told him, in Spanish, to stop touching my bags. In spite, he put his hand on my bag again. I motioned that I was going to remove him physically from my bag. He grabbed one of the zippers on my bags and started playing with it. I grabbed his hand and pulled it away. He complained that I hurt his hand. The boys all backed up and looked surprised and scared. They were staring at me not knowing what to do. They quickly all left. I now expect this type of behavior at border crossings. It's where travelers congregate and thieves look for opportunities.

After a few more minutes, Cindie returned with a pile of papers that she was filling out and a man who was supposed to inspect our bikes. She was annoyed but kept her voice calm end even managed a pretend smile. The official man wrote down the serial number from the bottom of my bike and then did the same with Cindie's bike. Cindie told me that this was necessary for our vehicle permit. I asked her (in English) how much our vehicle permit was going to cost. The official answered me in English "nothing." I was glad that I hadn't said anything negative. We never knew who would understand English. He and Cindie went back into the office. A different official man came around looking into everyone's trunk and inside of luggage. He looked at our bikes and me for a long time but never searched us. We had nothing to hide, but being searched would be no fun.

After another half hour, I saw Cindie emerge from the Nicaraguan office with our passports and a handful of papers. She announced that we could go now. She laughed and told me, "The good news is that we have a ninety day tourist visa. The bad news is that our bikes only have a thirty day vehicle permit." Cindie had tried to change this, but the officials didn't see the point. In the end we went on our merry way; we didn't plan to stay in Nicaragua for more than thirty days anyway.

We took our traditional border-crossing picture and rode up to the final gate. The border guard there checked every paper Cindie had filled out and had stamped. He also checked our passports for the exit stamp from Honduras and entry stamp into Nicaragua. He lifted the gate and down the Nicaraguan road we went. We coasted downhill for twenty-nine kilometers (eighteen miles) on a great newly-paved road to Ocotal, Nicaragua.

Looking back on the ordeal, I wondered which was worse, the US$10 we had to pay to "grease the palm" of the Honduran exit stamp man or the US$14 in official fees and the one hour of paperwork time it had taken to enter Nicaragua.

Deep In Sandinista Territory

Before entering a new country, we always read about its history and political climate. I find it interesting how a guidebook written by British or Australian authors paint a different picture about the USA's involvement in these countries than books written by an author from the U.S. My history books in school apparently had omitted parts of the story, especially when the USA was the villain. We read about the Sandinista uprising and the scandal that had unfolded a few years after that uprising in our guidebook. You may remember the "Iran Contra Scandal." We were riding in the northern part of Nicaragua where much of the ugly story had played out.

As soon we crossed into northern Nicaragua, we noticed a tension in the air. The Sandinista or FSLN had signs, slogans and billboards. They were still a popular and strong political party in northern Nicaragua. This didn't bother me. What bothered me was the graffiti. This wasn't from a political party but from the mind-set of people who had suffered so greatly. Nicaraguans are well known for their poetry, and much of the graffiti was in the form of poetry and cartoons. Sometimes it expressed pure hate. A common theme was a burning American flag or Uncle Sam hung from a tree. The air was tense, and I didn't dare take a picture of such images. We kept a low profile and acted as if we didn't notice the graffiti.

Because of the USA's involvement in the war and the obvious resentment in this area, we hadn't been sure how the locals would receive a couple from the USA. After seeing things painted on buildings, we had a good idea. We did what many other red-blooded Americans would do in this situation. We told people that we were from Canada. This isn't a game here. We were exposed and vulnerable traveling on bicycles, and we were in an unknown situation. We met many people whose sons and fathers had been killed because of something we called a scandal in the USA.

Riding In a Troubled Land

Along the road from the border to the small city of Ocotal, we saw several inviting places to camp; however, both of our guidebooks repeatedly warned of the numerous live land mines leftover from the war. People we had met warned us not to stray from the road while in northern Nicaragua. We even saw a few people with missing limbs.

243

Few foreigners stop in Ocotal. We rode around town looking for a room. The locals stopped what they were doing and stared. They were suspicious and even unfriendly. This didn't give us a good feeling, but we understood why. I wanted to talk to them and have the same friendly conversations we had grown accustomed to in Latin America.

I looked in a few bike shops for bicycle chain oil. I had used most of my bicycle chain oil during the weeks of wet weather in Honduras. I always love to visit bike shops during our travels. We were immediately accepted and understood. The bond of loving the same sport creates immediate friendships. This was true even in this unfriendly town. The guys who worked in the shop and the kids who hung out there all gathered around to meet us. Introductions and hearty handshakes were exchanged. They were surprised to see Cindie on her bike. They could understand me traveling by bicycle, but when they met Cindie, they couldn't believe that a woman would travel this way. It doesn't make sense in their male dominated world. The women, on the other hand, showed interest by crowding around Cindie. They saw Cindie as an example of a woman's equality in other parts of the world. Unfortunately, they kept quiet whenever the men were around.

The guys in the shop closely examined every component on our bikes. They counted the number of sprockets in our gearing (nine) and marveled at our clipless pedals. After a long talk about our trip and bikes, I learned that people in this part of the world use regular motor oil on their bicycle chain. The concept of special oil for a bicycle wasn't going to be understood in this small town. I still had a little of my bicycle chain oil that I had brought from Arizona and hoped that I could make it last until Costa Rica. I had heard that modern bikes and bike shops were abundant there.

We found a hotel and settled in. Later that day we met Alejandro while walking around the town square. He was a university student from the town of Leon. We had heard that Nicaraguans were passionate about life and politics. Alejandro fit this description completely. He started in quickly after our introduction speaking freely after we had told him we were Canadians. He was a proud member of the Sandinista party and didn't like Americans. He told us this several times. We later learned that he had never actually met any Americans. This didn't stop him from telling us how terrible they were. When I asked him why, he answered that he hated America because they had promoted and funded a war that had brought so much destruction to his people. What could I say? If I were in his place, I would probably feel the same way. We talked for several hours.

Esteli, Nicaragua

From Ocotal we had a long and mountainous ride to Esteli. Because of the land mine danger, we were afraid to camp. Esteli, and the area around it, had the hardest fighting during the war. The town was the last place to fall, and the people that lived there were proud of this fact. Esteli had several murals around town that depicted the heroes of the various battles and reminders of their ideologies. I was able to take several good pictures of these murals. The emotions of these people lived on their walls. I never felt comfortable taking these pictures because of the deeper political meaning.

Every American should see the Sandinista museum in Esteli. A group of mothers who had lost their sons during the war ran it. The walls were covered with pictures of young men who were gone, thousands of them. The caretaker on duty asked if we would like to see her son's picture. How could we say no? She slowly walked over and pointed at a color picture of a man who looked to be in his early 20's. She had a tear in her eye when she told us the story of the day of his death. The city had been surrounded by enemy forces and was under siege. The Sandinista fighters had built a

Mural on the wall in Esteli.

perimeter around Esteli out of construction materials and landscaping blocks. Artillery shells had been exploding everywhere inside the city. No place had been safe. The men had prayed together and promised to fight to the last one alive. Framed pictures on the wall showed what might have been this defensive structure and hungry frightened men defending it. She said many more emotional things that my Spanish couldn't handle. I didn't dare ask her to repeat anything. She was suffering enough reliving that day. In the end, he never came home and the city fell several days later. As she was pointing at the wall of pictures, she said, "None of these boys ever came home." She also said that he had been about my age (he actually looked ten years younger) and while looking tenderly at Cindie, she sadly said, "He never had time to marry."

From Esteli we climbed a couple of hours to a point overlooking Lake Managua. The only place that we could find to

Cindie looking at photos of men who died in the war.

sit and rest was a grave site with a crypt. According to the inscription, the two men had died nearby during the war.

After our lunch of cheese and tortilla, we coasted downhill for at least twenty-five kilometers (sixteen miles). When we were done with the mountains, we found ourselves on Nicaragua's hot coastal plain. We were less than one-hundred meters (328 feet) above sea level, and the air felt like it was coming out of a blow dryer. It would take several uncomfortable weeks before we acclimated to such heat. I still prefer the cool mountains.

This wasn't like the tropical heat that we had previously encountered in the jungle of southern Mexico. We were in a desert; the hillsides were barren of trees, and the air was dry. It brought back memories of the desert parts of Arizona. The road turned and went through an irrigated valley where the locals grew rice. The wind blew in our faces and our pace

247

fell considerably. We were hot and tired and didn't feel like fighting a headwind of about fifteen mph (twenty-four kph).

As luck would have it, an old farm tractor passed us. I learned a useful technique while growing up in Indiana: I learned how to draft off slow moving farm machinery. Drafting, for a cyclist, is the art of riding close enough behind something to have it block the wind. Usually a cyclist drafts off another cyclist, which makes riding 30% easier. I'm not sure how much of an advantage drafting off a tractor is, but it definitely is easier. Cindie, who usually drafts off me anyway, pulled up next to me behind the tractor. Our speed doubled and our effort decreased. This may not be the most politically correct habit, but it was what we needed at the end of a long hot day.

Once we were behind the tractor, I dropped back and pulled the camera out of my handle bar bag. I took a good picture of Cindie riding behind that tractor. I almost didn't

Cindie drafting behind a farm tractor.

make it back behind the tractor because I was out of the draft.

We followed that tractor for ten kilometers (six miles) until we saw a hotel. It was getting late, and this was the first hotel that we had seen in hours on this desolate road. We let the tractor go and pulled in for the night.

Peter the Dutch Cyclist

It was at this hotel that we met Peter, an experienced bicycle tourist. Peter was nearing sixty years old and showed no signs of slowing down. He had graying hair that had seen dozens of helmets during the last half century and knotted muscular legs from countless kilometers in the saddle. He had been to every country that I could think of, and many he had ridden through several times. This wasn't his first time riding through Nicaragua.

He had come from the direction that we were going. He told us about what we were going to encounter. We knew the roads and mountains that he was about to ride through. We invited him into our room for an evening of looking at maps and listening to his wonderful stories of his years of roaming the globe on a bike.

Peter had no email and no other way of ever contacting him again. He told me that he was moving soon and would be getting a new phone number in Holland. He was gone the next day before the sun came up. I wondered if he was real.

It took us two days to travel the 125 kilometers (78 miles) to Granada in 90° Fahrenheit (32° Celsius) heat. As we rode, we could see several volcanoes along the horizon. One of them was smoking. Cindie explained to me why all the volcanoes were lined up. Something to do with one tectonic plate being subducted below another tectonic plate in this area. I called this part of Nicaragua "Volcano Alley."

We rode past several different types of farms and the people who work on them. We had left the Sandinista area and were again telling people that we were from the United States. The people here were happy to see us spinning along. People went out of their way to talk to us and make us feel welcome. The USA had helped them win their civil war. It's crazy how things can change in a few kilometers.

Granada, Nicaragua

As we rode into Granada, we were impressed with the colonial architecture. From my bike, I saw one historical building after another. Granada was built in the late 1800's and early 1900's, and the colonial buildings were detailed and decorative although some buildings were falling apart.

We pulled into the picturesque main plaza and cooled off in the shade. We must have looked travel weary and hot. Two Canadian retirees bought us ice cream and told us about the area. I met several more people while Cindie found us a place to stay.

As we talked, I noticed three homeless kids sniffing jars of glue. This very disturbing behavior was a big problem all over Central America. Instead of playing soccer or doing their homework, they were stumbling around the plaza with paper bags pressed against their faces inhaling toxic chemicals. We were aware that kids were addicted to glue, but this was the first time that we actually saw them openly inhaling the toxic fumes. They made no effort to hide this behavior, and these kids asked us repeatedly for money.

We stayed in a downtown hostel for almost a week. We met the usual mixture of short-term travelers, international drifters and hard-core long-term travelers. Many had already circled the globe and were on round two. I find that people who love to travel are interesting and are generally a knowledge-seeking group. They had been to places around

Main square of colonial Granada.

the world that we plan to go and have elaborate stories to tell. They never stopped looking for answers or wondering what is around the next corner. I talked with a group of people from Switzerland, Scotland and other parts of the world late into the night. Their stories were better than any television show.

In Granada, we did a lot of walking around and looking at old buildings. I loved studying the history of the place. We also went on several day trips to nearby attractions, sat for hours in the lovely downtown park and even went to the dentist.

Volcano Masaya

We took a day trip from Granada to the Volcano Masaya. We rode a bus to the national park and hitchhiked to the top. From the top, we had big views of the whole area. We could also look into its many craters and see smoke coming out of the main crater. We were surprised to see so little smoke because this same volcano had emitted a large plume of smoke a few days before. A volcano can be like a living person; its mood changes every day. The landscape had a lunar look and feel. We hiked around one of the extinct craters and eventually back down the five kilometers (three miles) to the entrance. From there we caught a bus back to Granada.

Nicaraguan Dentist

Many people think that outside of the first world there is nothing but "witch doctors." This isn't true. Modern health care can be found in most large cities throughout the world. In Granada, Nicaragua, we decided to visit a local dentist. We both needed a good cleaning and Cindie had pain from a couple cavities that required attention. Several months earlier, before we had left Arizona, I would have never dreamed of seeing a dentist in Nicaragua. Now, many kilometers later, I had a better understanding of how things worked in a country like Nicaragua. The majority of people are very poor and cannot afford a dentist. A small percentage of the population has a substantial amount of money. They have new trucks and satellite TV; their kids attend expensive, private bilingual schools, and they regularly see modern dentists and doctors with the same equipment as the first world nations. This means that all of the health care and other professional services are available in the larger cities.

The dentist that we saw had all of the same equipment that you would find in developed countries. We felt comfortable getting a professional cleaning, and Cindie had a couple cavities filled, it cost US$60. I probably wouldn't have had something more serious, like a root canal or a bridge, done. It's not because I think our Nicaraguan dentist was incompetent. It's because our dentist didn't speak much English, and our Spanish isn't up to dental surgery. It's hard enough to speak English with all of that stuff in your mouth.

Horses were dressed in ornamental bridles and saddles.

The Country Horse Show

During our time in Granada, we were lucky enough to stumble across a local "cowboy" festival after meeting another tourist, Joe, on our way to an internet cafe. The next thing we knew we were in a cab and speeding off to a nearby village.

Many people in Nicaragua raise cattle on large ranches and are proud of their fine horses. I think that this is one of the better legacies left over from the Spanish.

In this small village, everyone who had a special or nice looking horse was riding it in the street. The streets were so crowded with horses that it was difficult to walk or drive a car. The horses danced down the street and were dressed elaborately with leather strings hanging from their saddles and bridles. There were live bands on every corner, clowns performing in the street and a carnival with an old unstable

253

Ferris wheel.

Joe, Cindie and I were the only non-Nicaraguan people in the large crowd. People did double takes when they heard us speaking Spanish in our thick American accents. I loved it. The locals appreciated the fact that we were interested in witnessing their special festival. Most went out of their way to make us feel welcome. I had to turn down dozens of free beers but accepted many heartfelt handshakes. When we were making introductions, I was never sure if the names were for the horse or rider. This kind of off-the-beaten track cultural gathering is the best way to learn about how people live in a certain region.

To Ride or Not To Ride (The Ferry)

We had plans to go to Isla Ometepe, located across Lake Nicaragua, on a ferryboat. On the day we planned to leave, the winds blew stronger than usual. When it comes to boat travel, Lake Nicaragua behaves more like a sea than a lake. When Cindie went to the ferry dock, she reported that the lake was covered with white caps. This would mean a rough five-hour ferry ride to the island. There was another option. We could ride our bikes 75 kilometers (47 miles) around the lake to San Jorge and take a one-hour ferry ride to the island from there. Since I easily get motion sick, we decided to ride our bikes the 75 kilometers (47 miles) to San Jorge.

After a long and windy ride, we arrived at the boat dock. Still, the lake looked rough; at least now it was only a one-hour ferry ride to Isla Ometepe. We waited until a banana boat unloaded two truckloads of bananas. I pushed my bike up to the boat and saw no way to get it on. Then a man laid an old wooden plank from the boat to the dock. The plank moved up and down with the waves of the lake. Before I had time to say, "Are you crazy," they had grabbed my bike and began pushing it across the plank. For a brief

Tim's bike being loaded on the boat to Ometepe.

Vendor selling fruit at the boat dock in San Jorge.

moment my bike tiptoed across the plank and was inches away from falling into the rough waters of Lake Nicaragua. Forever lost. I saw this as a big risk and a potential end of our lifelong dream to bike tour around the world. Cindie's bike was loaded in much the same way. Both bikes made it safely across the plank to the boat. The ancient diesel engine started, and we were on our way. Immediately the boat pitched back and fourth. I was grateful for my Dramamine while I sat at the front of the boat rocking from side to side and waiting for the ride to end. Everyone else enjoyed the scenery. We arrived in Moyogalpa, the largest city on Isla Ometepe, an hour later.

Isla Ometepe

The 8,624 square kilometer (5,390 square mile) fresh water Lake Nicaragua surrounds the large island of Ometepe. Two volcanoes, Maderas and Concepcion that are joined together by lava flows, form this island. It's an off-road cyclist's dream. It has much of the same appeal as the San Juan Islands in Washington State, USA: flat-ish roads (dirt) with little traffic and many scenic routes. Many trails meander among the coffee fields and connect car-free villages to palm-lined beaches. Numerous birds and monkeys were in the trees. The locals were friendly.

On the island, we noticed a rural way of life. Men rode horses, and oxen pulled squeaky homemade carts down the roads. Barefoot kids used old coconuts to play rowdy games of soccer, I don't believe that there was one street sign or house number on the entire island.

We stayed in Moyogalpa for five days. The power went out almost every evening, but no one seemed to care.

In other parts of Latin America, we had seen countless stray dogs. On the Island of Ometepe we had seen stray pigs and horses as well. Seeing a group of five horses walking freely around town poking through trash and small gardens

Volcano Concepcion on the Island of Ometepe.

was something I had never seen before. I asked a shop owner who owned the horses and he answered, "Some things are meant to be free."

Climbing Volcano Maderas

We decided to hike up Volcano Maderas the next day with a group of people we had met at dinner. At 6:30 a.m. we met Phil from Canada, Tanya from Germany, Brad from Australia and Bart from Holland in front of Hospedaje Central where they were staying. Because buses weren't running that early in the morning, we all chipped in on a cab that would take us straight to the trailhead at Finca Magdalena where we decided to have breakfast.

Cindie and I had heard that a guide was unnecessary, but the others in the group wanted one, so we hired a man from a nearby village for $4 per person. This was extremely expensive in that country. Our guide, Leo, carried only a small amount of water, a pack of cigarettes, matches and a machete that he kept slung over his back. He was a wiry fellow that was muscular and didn't have an ounce of fat on him. He spoke Spanish with a thick accent that suggested that his time in school had been cut short by the need to work. We later learned that he had led hikes up and down the volcano every other day for the last several years.

We left the finca and started climbing among coffee fields and production areas. We soon entered a dense dry forest. Leo showed us petroglyphs carved in rock and posed for a few pictures. He also pointed out a group of monkeys, a termite nest and various plants and animals as we climbed up the side of the steep volcano. At one point Leo turned around with a serious look on his face and announced that we were about to enter the wet rain forest. I don't think that any of us believed that it was going to be wet because we were walking on a dry and dusty trail.

Brad and Phil stuck in the mud.

Tim, Brad and Phil climbing out of Volcano Maderas.

Suddenly the vegetation changed and the ground became moist and muddy. In the beginning, we tried to tiptoe around the deep mud and keep our shoes clean. This became impossible, as all of the ground became ankle deep in mud. We were squishing along at a labored and slow pace. This wasn't your typical mud. It consisted of slippery wet clay that clung to our shoes in big clumps. At one point, Brad pulled his foot up and his shoe remained submerged in the mud. We all stopped and tied our shoes tighter. A couple of

259

hours of this went by and still the summit was way off. Leo had no trouble and danced through the mud while the rest of us stumbled and slid. During a rest stop, I told Leo that he was strong. He replied, "I have to be, I am Nicaraguan." I believe that he meant more than physically strong.

When we finally reached the top of the crater, we asked Leo where the lookout was. We all had thought that it would be possible to see the entire Lake Nicaragua and beyond to the Pacific Ocean. Leo told us that there was no such view place and that the dense vegetation made it impossible to see far. After several hours of hard work, we were all expecting the payoff to be a grand view. We saw nothing but moss-covered trees and took pictures of that instead. The area certainly had its own beauty and unique environment.

From the rim of the crater, we started descending down to the lake below. It was so steep and treacherous that one wrong move would have meant a serious fall. We had to use a rope to climb down a sheer cliff. At the bottom of the crater was a small lake, ringed by rain forest vegetation that clung to the side of the extinct volcano.

We took a group picture, and then sat down to eat lunch. Leo announced that we would be leaving in one hour and immediately fell asleep under a shade tree. We couldn't believe how tired and muddy we all were, and we knew the day was only half over. When our break was done, we climbed back up the rope and then started the long descent down the muddy trail. Believe it our not, going down was much harder than going up. Brad, Phil and I slipped and fell in the mud, which added to our overall filthiness. Once we descended below the wet forest, the sun beat down upon us and the mud on our bodies hardened like clay pots in a kiln. When we reached the finca, all of us were beyond exhaustion and couldn't walk another step. We had been hiking for over eight hours.

Nicaragua: Sandinistas and Contras

View of Volcano Concepcion from Chaco Verde.

Local boy riding on the beach.

Then another adventure began. Sadly, we learned that public transportation is nonexistent on Sunday evenings on this rural island. We asked if we could call a cab, but apparently the phone wasn't functioning. We then asked if there was a phone in the nearby village. We learned that most people don't even have electricity, and a telephone was out of the question. We all gathered our strength and walked another half hour down the road to a primitive village. We thought we could either hail a cab or hitch a ride with a passing vehicle.

When we reached the main road that rings the island, it was void of traffic. This is a cyclist's dream and a hitchhiker's nightmare. We reluctantly walked on down the road looking for any form of transportation. We came across a jeep and a pickup truck parked next to a candle lit pool hall. We spoke to several men watching the setting sun and drinking warm beer. The jeep didn't run and the pickup truck belonged to the mayor.

The mayor was summoned. When he came out of the house he found an exhausted group of foreigners covered head-to-toe in mud. He laughed when we told him we were trying to get a ride to Moyogalpa. Apparently, none of the locals would attempt this on a Sunday. He said he would drive us to the nearby town of Santa Domingo and try to find us a ride to the other side of the island. We were impressed to learn that he was also the mayor of that town. When we thanked him in advance for his help, he said, "I want you to remember your visit to the Island of Ometepe well." I thought that was hospitable of him.

In Santa Domingo, he stopped at his house and went inside to find us a ride to Moyogalpa. As we were sitting in the back of the truck, we heard what must have been the only other vehicle in operation ramble closer. Bart waved down the truck and learned that they were heading to Chaco Verde, twelve kilometers (7.4 miles) from Moyogalpa. Close enough for now. During the ride to Chaco Verde, the truck stalled on a short, but steep hill. We all had to get out and push. The truck took off to the top of the hill and we had to run. By the time we reached Chaco Verde, Bart had talked the driver into taking us all the way to our hotels in Moyogalpa.

It took several showers to wash off all of the dried mud, and I was sore for at least five days after the hike. If I could turn back time, I would have voted to skip this particular hike. It was an incredible amount of hard work without a view from the top.

Ernie the Musical Sensation from Jamaica

There was so little motorized traffic on Ometepe it was common to sit or play soccer in the streets. The breeze was better in the open. The power had gone out again, and the moon and a few candles were the only dependable sources of light.

I saw a foreign man sitting out in the street. This person had long flowing dreadlocks and a friendly demeanor. I knew that he had a story to tell and that I had to meet him. I walked up to him and said "good evening" in Spanish. He answered me back in English with a friendly "Well, good evening to you." The rest of our conversation was in English. He was Ernic Smith, a professional musician and performer from Jamaica. Usually if someone tells me that he is a professional singer, I would be skeptical. You hear many tall tales on the road. It turned out that Ernie was telling the truth. We talked for a long time while we watched a group of kids play soccer in the moonlight. He had been all over the world with his music. When the night grew late, we parted company.

The evening before we were going to leave the island, the electricity went out again. Cindie and I were walking down the dark street and found Ernie watching a group of kids playing. He invited us to sit down and have a local beer. He found seats for us and we joined him and his family.

We were introduced to Ernie's son, Adrian, and his wife Jane. Jane was also Ernie's manager, and they were in Ometepe to visit their son. Adrian had put a prosperous career as an attorney on hold to become a Peace Corp Volunteer. This struck me as an unselfish act and earned my deepest respect. We spoke to him at length about his experiences in the Peace Corp. So far, we have never met anyone who has had a bad experience.

Next, a local singer/song writer named Oscar showed up with two acoustic guitars. He gave one to Ernie. Ernie handled the battered instrument as if he had played it for years. He fixed a broken string then he completely tuned it by ear. When Ernie started playing, I had no doubt that he had played all of his life. He came alive and showed a true love for his craft. Ernie could play all kinds of music including Reggae; he could also play American country and knew every Johnny Cash song that I could name. Ernie has a long list of songs that he has written and even numerous CDs that sell well in Jamaica and throughout the world.

Oscar quickly joined in playing acoustic duets with Ernie. He was talented as well. He sat where he could see Ernie's hands so he could follow along. Oscar sang the songs that he had written. He had a couple songs that I thought could easily be chart toppers in the Spanish-speaking world. The two played together late into the night as if they were old friends.

We learned that Ernie was going to perform a free concert for the people living in the area. This was too good to pass up so we decided to stay an extra night.

The next day Cindie and I went on a bike ride around the roads on the island. Everyone we met told us about the free concert. Word travels fast in such a small community. When we returned to Moyogalpa, everyone was waiting for the big show. It's not every day that such a famous and professional performer comes to an isolated island in Nicaragua.

That evening the concert started late because of another power outage. Time has a much different relevance in Latin America. No one expected the show to start any earlier than it did anyway. Ernie had an impressive electronic sound system set up in the town's combination basketball court and soccer field. There was a crowd of about one hundred people there. Once a few technical bugs were worked out of the system, Ernie started playing. He was an excellent performer. We heard the same songs as in the private acoustic concert the night before.

I am certain that many people on this island had never seen anyone play an electric guitar before, much less a complete Las Vegas-quality show. Ernie was rocking out and the crowd stared in admiration.

Eventually they talked Oscar into going up on stage. Every local on this island knew Oscar and his music. Several days before we had met him, we had seen him playing to a bunch of little kids while sitting on his front porch steps. It had been like a scene from an old Saturday Evening Post cover.

When Oscar sang his song about his country life on Isla Ometepe, the crowd knew every word and sang along. It was great to see the "small town boy make it big" even if it was for fifteen minutes.

On To a New Country

The boat ride back to the mainland was rough. Because we had to ride sixty kilometers (37 miles) and get through another dreaded international border, I wanted all of my strength. Dramamine, the anti-motion sick pills that I usually take, would make me sleepy and worthless for the rest of the day. I rode the boat without it, and I nearly had to hang my head over the side and "feed the fish." When I got off the boat, I could barely walk. Cindie had to supervise the unloading of the bikes and keep watch for the usual pickpockets that hang out in such places. At that point, I didn't care if someone jumped on my bike and rode away. Cindie dragged our two rigs and me to a shady spot. This gave me time to shake off my motion sickness. A carbonated soda appeared to help. I couldn't sit long because it grew hot, and we wanted to ride while it was still relatively cool.

The ride to the Costa Rican border was scenic. The Pan America road is next to Lake Nicaragua for a long way. We had a couple hours to view distant volcanoes and contemplate life of the Nicaraguans who live in the dozens of small villages along the shore. By the time we reached the international border, I was more or less recovered from my bout of motion sickness and was eager to enter Costa Rica.

Cindie passing a cart pulled by oxen.

13 Costa Rica: Monkeys, Iguanas and Surfers

(February 21 – April 11, 2003)

We had heard for weeks before entering Costa Rica that the border was a real nightmare. We were prepared for an all day border crossing, waiting in lines and untangling red tape.

We had to visit several offices to get all of our exit stamps to leave Nicaragua. We then rode up to the Costa Rican Immigration official to get our entry stamps into Costa Rica. We most dreaded this part.

I found a comfortable place outside the office to sit and watch the bikes, and Cindie went in to deal with the red tape. It was mid-afternoon and over 90° Fahrenheit (32° Celsius). Anticipating a long wait, we had made sure that each of us had water and food.

The first thing that I noticed about Costa Rica was the absence of pickpockets milling around looking for opportunities. Instead, I found myself talking to a group of Costa Ricans in a motorcycle club who were riding around Central America on their fancy Harley Davidson motorcycles. The differences in economies between Costa Rica and the countries to the north –Nicaragua, Honduras and Guatemala – were already noticeable. These leather-clad bikers were friendly. I jokingly offered to trade my bicycle for one of their expensive noisemakers. One of the guys even acted like he was considering the trade and walked around my bicycle to inspect it. He said that he liked that I had more luggage than he did and the lack of licenses plates, police stops and lower maintenance made the deal more appealing. He finally shrugged his shoulders and said that although he was tempted he couldn't do it. He said that he would miss the thunder in the tail pipe, the smell of exhaust and his big belly too much. Then he immediately pulled his shirt up to expose his prize that must have taken years to grow. We all had a big laugh.

Before I finished my conversation with the motor bikers, Cindie walked out with a smile on her face. She said that we were done and ready to go. I didn't believe her because she had been gone only for fifteen minutes, and the officials hadn't even seen me. They had only seen my passport. She showed me the stamps, and we rode to the gate at the border. The man there took a quick look at the stamps in our passports. He noticed that we had traveled overland from the USA and asked us how far we were going south. We enthusiastically answered in unison "Argentina." He gave us thumbs up, opened the gate and down the Costa Rican road we went.

From the border, we had a hot ride in the afternoon sun to our first Costa Rican town of La Cruz. There were a couple of checkpoints, but the officers who stopped us wanted to talk and pass time. They never asked to see our passports. Instead, they wanted to know of all of the places that we had been and where we were going. Talking to them was a lot of fun, but we had to get moving. I think they were sad to see us go.

After a ten kilometer (six mile) climb into town, we were covered in sweat. The further south we rode the hotter it was getting. We pulled into the main plaza, and Cindie bought ice cream from a nearby store. It was our first experience with Costa Rican money and high prices. We had been used to similar exchange rates in all of the previous countries. These exchange rates had ranged from 7.5 quetzales to one US dollar in Guatemala to seventeen lempiras to one US dollar in Honduras. The exchange rate when we entered Costa Rica was 384 colonies to one US dollar. This high number doesn't stop things from costing more. Our two ice creams cost about one thousand colonies or about US$2.60. Except for Mexico, which is also relatively expensive, two ice creams would have cost about US$0.75 in the countries we had visited to the north.

We asked each other, "How are we ever going to survive here on our budget?" Time would tell. We asked a taxi driver where the cheap hotels were and he gave us directions. We rode the short distance, settled into our first Costa Rican room for 3,500 colonies (US$9.12), and reflected on the differences in this new country.

Differences

Costa Rica is doing much better economically compared to Guatemala, Honduras and Nicaragua. This makes things more expensive, but also brings welcome changes.

Places are cleaner because of organized garbage pick up service and numerous public trash cans around town. Costa Ricans are also proud of their beautiful country and don't like to leave their trash on the ground.

The police were professional looking and abundant in numbers. They smiled and waved at us. This and the general mood of the people made everything feel and look much more secure. We decided that we could now dig our wedding rings from the hidden place in the bottom of Cindie's bag and put them back on our fingers. We hadn't had them on since our first day in Guatemala when we had noticed that the impoverished population there immediately noticed the gold bands.

Another convenience was refrigeration. We had grown accustomed to seeing meat hanging in open-air shops. The meats we saw for sale in this small town were wrapped in plastic and neatly placed in grocery style cooling units.

There were a few things that were worse compared to the countries to the north. The dogs were domesticated and well fed. This isn't a problem in itself, but the happy dogs usually

269

had the job of guarding the farm or yard in front of the family house. For some unknown reason these dogs regularly saw Cindie and me as a severe threat to their territory and gave chase. The battle was on again. This war has surely been waged since the invention of the bicycle.

The dogs came running out with as many friends as were available to bark, snarl and threaten to bite us. I, in response, spit, yell and show my teeth. If this doesn't work, I begin a weaving motion on my bike with the goal of catching the lead dog exposed, and then I try to sprint to ramming speed. Rarely do I make contact, but the aggressive action usually convinces them to back down. We kept saying that we were going to get rocks or dog treats to throw during dog attacks.

The traffic increased in Costa Rica as well. In the countries to the north, even on the main roads, vehicles were always few and far between. To make things worse, the roads were in much worse shape. Big holes were common and the road turned to gravel without warning. At least this kept the speed of the traffic down.

<u>Unlikely Oasis</u>

We overslept in our comfortable room and started late. We rolled out of town at 8:15 a.m. It was already over 80° Fahrenheit (26.5° Celsius), and I had a layer of sweat developing on my skin. We knew that it was going to get worse.

We rode past expansive ranch land and serious Costa Rican cowboys going about their business of raising cattle. After 9 a.m., we noticed that all of the cowboys had disappeared. They knew when to get out of the heat. We still had a long way to go, and the hot sun was beating the life out of us. Such heat makes exercise dangerous, but we had to keep going. We made numerous stops and tried to let the dry hot wind cool us, but it could only do so much. Heat waves blurred the black road.

Hours later, I knew we should be close to our next town. However, we saw nothing but ranch land and wild bananas. I was starting to think that I had misread the map or miscalculated the distance. It was now 11 a.m. and over 95° Fahrenheit (35° Celsius), dangerously hot for riding a bike. Cindie doesn't do as well in the heat as I do, and I was starting to get dizzy. I knew that she was probably close to getting seriously sick. It was THAT hot. She was sitting tight in my draft so conversation was easy although we spoke seldom on this stretch. I asked, "How are you doing?" and received a garbled reply stating that the end was near. We rode on in silence.

Then I thought I heard Cindie say "Burger King," I asked her to repeat herself and she said "Burger King" again. I was suddenly concerned for her health. I thought of different ways of cooling her down. I looked around and didn't see any

Heat waves blurred the black road.

shade, and I also knew that we were running low on water.

Cindie said, "I really do see a Burger King."

I looked up the road and saw the big yellow sign that announced the American fast food giant. We instantly pulled in, and we both quickly noticed that there were no open windows. I said, "Cindie, I think that they have air conditioning in there!"

Cindie began to cry. We hadn't seen air conditioning since Villahermosa, Mexico about six months before. I could tell that Cindie was dizzy because she dropped her bike and had trouble walking in. I locked the bikes together and joined her.

All eyes in the restaurant were on us. We must have looked half-dead. When the cold air hit me, it felt like another world. It was too good to be true. We ordered big drinks and food. I have always loved Whoppers and fries. The smell

Cindie at the Burger King in Liberia, Costa Rica.

reminded me of the time I worked at a Burger King when I was in high school.

We sat in the artificially cooled (65° Fahrenheit, 18.5° Celsius) building for three hours. We slowly ate and drank about a gallon (3.78 liters) of pop each. When we finally cooled down enough to grow goose bumps, we decided to head into the city of Liberia to see what excitement awaited us there.

Liberia, Costa Rica

Liberia was our first city of substantial size in Costa Rica. We stuck to our tried and true plan of first finding the main plaza, getting our bearings and then sending Cindie to compare room prices while I watched our loaded bikes. My job of watching our gear was much easier in this modern secure country. Out of habit, I scanned the crowd looking for any suspicious characters. Instead of coming up with my top three people to keep an eye on, I saw nobody that looked suspicious. Many people would stop and ask where we had come from or what our nationality was but no one scanned our bikes trying to figure out where we kept our valuables.

I struck up a conversation with the guys on the bench next to me. They told me that they were from San Jose (the capital) and were in town for the famous two-week horse and bull festival. They looked like they were out to have a good time. One of the men had a particularly strange sense of humor. He picked up a bug crawling on the ground and asked me if I thought that he should eat it. I think he was asking me if I "dared" him to eat the bug in his hand, but I had never heard this word in Spanish before. I stalled in my reply not knowing what to say. Without receiving my answer, he threw the large bug in his mouth and chased it with a warm beer. His friends and I began laughing hysterically. Two old women sitting nearby looked disgusted, and a group of boys asked him to do it again.

Cindie returned from her hotel search and found the entire scene confusing. We pushed our bikes a couple blocks from the plaza and checked into a hotel. The only room that we could afford in Liberia was on the third floor and had a weak fan. The afternoon heat was terrible. I called the owner and told him that we needed another fan because this one made no breeze. He told me that the fan was fine. To prove my point I lit a match and held it in front of the fan. It didn't even flicker. He grabbed my burning match, ignited a cheap cigarette from a pack in his shirt pocket and promised to let me use the lobby fan during the night. At least we might be able to get some sleep.

By the time we had carried all of our bike bags up the stairs we were covered in sweat and overheating again. The only relief was to stand under the shared shower down the hall. All of the showers that our meager budget allowed in this hot climate had one knob for cold water. These cheap accommodations usually didn't bother with a shower head. They had a threaded pipe sticking out of the wall or held in place with either hose clamps or bits of old coat hangers. The water was never that cold because nothing in this sweltering climate could possibly feel cold. It was at least cooler than our body temperatures and was the only relief from the heat. We took several showers a day. I called it, "the poor man's air conditioner".

After a sweaty night we were talking in the morning to the hotel manager and learned that Liberia was starting a two-week festival that day. He said that we were lucky to get a room. Sure enough, the hotel and town filled up and a big party was under way. We couldn't believe our luck.

This wasn't the kind of festival that was meant to attract foreign tourists. This was a local attraction. This area of Costa Rica is called Guancaste and is home to thousands of proud cowboys involved in the endless ranching life. I'm not sure why foreign tourists avoid such cultural events.

What interested the people of Guanacaste, Costa Rica was showing off stunning horses, horseback riding, incredible rope skills, livestock, bulls and generally all things cowboy. We decided to stay several days and check it out. Cindie found an event schedule and we saw several events a day including a daily parade of fine horses.

We were told that families might ride for days to get to this event to show their horses. Young men and women have few chances to mingle and date on the isolation of the ranch, so this was also a big social event. I saw phone numbers and email addresses being exchanged, mostly while on horseback. In the parades, whole families would be in their best clothing and mounted on their finest horses. Some of the kids were so little that they were tied to the saddle of a gentle horse to keep them from falling off.

The street was crowded with horses, and we had to know when to move to avoid being trampled. It was assumed that everyone in the crowd knew how to behave around horses. I had no practical experience with horses and had to follow Cindie's lead in this arena. To me, it was out of control, but Cindie told me that everyone had exceptional riding skills and knew what they were doing.

The local dress included polished boots, perfectly fitting Spanish style cowboy hats, new blue jeans, ornate shirts with leather fringe for decoration and an elaborate belt with a huge belt buckle. Almost every adult had a cell phone hanging from his or her belt. This made sense because Costa Rica isn't a poor country, and a cell phone would greatly improve efficiency on the ranch. The constant ringing was out of place to me, but not at all to them. It was now a part of the new cowboy culture.

Young child in the horse parade.

The highlight event was the "Running of the Bulls" or by the other name used "Bull Fight." I expected either what you see on TV from Spain where the bulls chase people down the street or a regular bullfight with a matador where the bull has no chance. This turned out to be something completely different and much more bizarre.

Not Just Another Bull Fight

We walked across town to the bull ring. There were temporary drinking bars and discos thrown up everywhere and

Horse parade.

people partying. Horses were commonly tied up, but most people preferred to do their drinking right on the horse.

When we arrived at the bull ring, we bought tickets to the evening events. Tickets were divided into two price ranges, Sun and Shade. When I asked what the difference was the woman looked at me as if I was born yesterday. A friendly man, seeing our confusion, dismounted from his Arabian and explained it to us. Half of the stadium was shaded from the hot afternoon sun, and the other half was in the sun. He said that we should sit in the shade because the "better" people sit there and because we might die in the sun. I have never cared about being with the "better" people, but the dying part caught my attention. We decided to pay extra to sit on the shady side of the stadium.

The stadium was big and filling up fast. Venders came around selling things to eat and drink. I bought frozen red Jell-O in a bag and rubbed it on my neck to cool down before eating it. The crowd was all seated, and a man came on a loud speaker and started talking about the evening's big events and all of the corporate sponsors that made it possible. He also told the crowd that if they were drunk not to sit near the edge of the stadium where they could fall and get hurt.

He now asked the participants to come into the ring and young men and even boys climbed down from the seats into the ring. Most of the men came from the Sun section; they were wearing red shirts and carrying bottles of beer and hard liquor. They appeared to be drunk. Now I think when the man had said that the "better" people sit on the shady side, he meant the people who weren't drunk or crazy or both.

The announcer made a long introduction of the first bull and rider. I didn't understand all of what he said because the sound quality was bad, but I gathered that the rider was from a small town in the middle of nowhere and the bull was big and mean. I understood "bull" and "rider", but I couldn't figure out what all the drunken guys in the ring were for.

Finally, the bull came out with a man hanging on for his life. His hat flew off in the first two seconds, and he flew even further in about three more. OK, now what?

Next, all of the drunken guys started taunting the bull trying to persuade this large and mad beast to chase them. They would yell, run by and slap it on the rear or throw things at the bull to get its attention. The bull chased, but never caught anyone although there were several near misses. Eventually, one guy running from the bull tripped over his own feet, and the bull hit his mark. This wasn't pretty or staged in any way. The bull crushed him into the ground with his strong head and then backed up to get a running start. This guy must have had good friends because several men rushed in to pull him away while others distracted the bull. Then two men rode out with lassos and showed off their roping skills as they lassoed the bull and pulled him out of the ring.

I asked the lady next to me what would happen to the bull now. I was expecting that he would be killed and fed to the poor, but instead she told me that he would be taken home to breed. In fact, he was worth more because he pummeled the guy in the ring. I said to Cindie, who was turning green from witnessing the carnage, "Wow, this is different than the bullfights I have seen before in Mexico." The bull often wins and then gets to go home a hero with the sole purpose of breeding.

We sat through at least a dozen more bulls. Some chased guys around, and several others were successful in injuring someone. A few guys were so injured that their motionless bodies were carried away on stretchers. Then there was a drunk guy who could barely stand. The bull singled him out

Crazy people in the bull ring.

Bull chasing a participant.

This bull got a little too close.

in the crowd and started sprinting hard. I saw his eyes open then "bam" he was knocked in the air and landed at least three meters (ten feet) away. He was done and carried away. My guess was that he was dead. No one could possibly have lived through that.

I am thick-skinned, but this was getting hard to watch. Cindie, who had usually kept her eyes shut, had enough and wanted to leave. We excused ourselves and walked out. Fat chance of ever talking Cindie into anything like that again. I (jokingly) told Cindie that I wanted to buy a bottle of rum, go back, and get in the ring. She told me "absolutely not." I laughed hard, and she finally figured out that it was a joke.

The next day we packed and left before sunrise in order to beat the heat. I hate riding early, but there is no other way to deal with the hot and humid conditions. The one advantage of riding early is that you get to see the sunrise from the bicycle as you are sailing down the road. To see the giant red blazing ball rise over the expansive Guanacaste landscape inspired admiration and terror. As it inched its way above the horizon we knew that it was only a matter of time before this striking thing became our enemy.

We made good time in the coolness of the morning, but when the heat of the day descended upon us, we stopped on the side of the road for a break. An old but lively woman in a summer dress and tennis shoes joined us in the shade. She told us about visiting her grandkids nearby. She was returning to Liberia where she lived. When one of the infrequent cars approached, she excused herself, walked to the road, and stuck her thumb out to hitchhike. It was like a scene from the movie "Easy Rider," but the actress had aged. The car zoomed by, and I think I heard her swear under her breath. She returned to her seat with a girlish enthusiasm and picked up the conversation where she had left off. I could have talked to this woman all day, but we still had to make Playa Tamarindo before it was so hot our brains boiled under our helmets. Next, a large gas delivery truck appeared from around the corner and was approaching fast. She excused herself again in a cute way that only an old lady could manage – "Deary me, here comes a good one" – and walked out to the road. She lowered her thumb to the road. I thought that there was no way that this big truck, probably behind schedule, was going to stop. How wrong I was. The beast made the most whining noise but rapidly came to a stop. The driver wasn't able to stop directly in front of her, but he backed the whole thing up until the passenger door was directly in front of the smiling lady. She could barley reach the door handle but managed to open the door and climb into the cab. The giant diesel engine revved up, and the driver finally jerked it into first gear. Just after second gear began, I saw her little hand, complete with fresh white tissue, waving good-bye to us. A scene I will not forget. The rest of the ride to Playa Tamarindo wasn't nearly as interesting as watching that old lady stop a giant truck with only her thumb.

Playa Tamarindo, Costa Rica

Arriving at our first beach in Costa Rica was exciting. We found a place to sit where we could see and hear the ocean. We were hot and dripping sweat, but we had made it. We had seen the ocean only once before on our long trip from Arizona – that was in Honduras and doesn't count because it rained while there. This beach was sunny and tropical. Girls rode one-speed beach cruiser bikes in bikinis, and groups of boys walked around with surfboards. The strange thing was that everyone looked foreign and spoke English as if they were from Kansas. Yes, we had finally found where the Americans were hiding. In the grocery store, a group of tourists in beach clothes spoke English to confused clerks. We found ourselves translating for them.

Costa Rica: Monkeys, Iguanas and Surfers

Cindie asked around and learned where the cheapest campground was located. We pedaled off to find the campground, set up our tent and went swimming in the ocean. We were happy to learn that our campground had a security guard; we felt more at ease leaving our belongings behind. We didn't know it at the time, but Costa Rica has a reputation for petty crime. This was one of the few times we could safely leave our belongings in a campground.

Playa Tamarindo is a world famous surfing beach. It was swarming with surfer dudes and chicks. I love it when people dedicate themselves to a sport to the extent that a subculture forms around it. I have seen the same thing in skiing and cycling. It may sound silly to dedicate your life to a sport at first, but it sure is better than the things people usually dedicate their lives to: money, power or working and paying bills.

Surfer.

Playa Tamarindo.

This beach had more to offer than big waves. Tamarindo is a tropical paradise with tall healthy palms gently swaying in the humid breeze and all manner of sea birds drifting around. Every palm tree in our campground had at least one large iguana crawling around it. These things look like they stepped out of the Stone Age. They are often the size of a typical house cat, but far uglier. The local Costa Rican name for an iguana (translated to English) is "tree chicken." This makes a lot of sense when you consider that it's common to eat iguanas. Believe me, there is no shortage.

Besides the surfer culture, the most interesting natural thing about this beach was the presence of various types of monkeys playing in the trees and on the rooftops. They are an unruly bunch and like to startle you with their loud noises or sudden movements. They are intelligent and curious. The monkeys live an easy life, and if they would learn to surf, I would consider their lifestyle perfect.

Tim riding along the coast of Costa Rica.

The Beach Less Traveled

Leaving Tamarindo began our long ride through the infrequently visited beaches on dirt roads. It was time to see how the locals lived and hear what they had to say. Our dirt road went past rural towns and small schools. It was slow hot going again, and our bodies were covered in sweat by 9:30 a.m., but the scenery was pleasant.

Towards the evening, we knocked on several doors and asked for water, but they all reported that the water system wasn't working. They always offered to fill our small water bottles, but they couldn't spare the ten liters (2.6 gallons) that it takes to fill our bag to camp in the bush. They always were concerned. Apparently, something was broken, and the water wasn't working for anyone.

We had no choice but to push on into the afternoon sun. When we reached Playa Largosta beach, we saw a small creek emptying into the ocean. We knew that this might have to do. The water was slow moving and murky. We hadn't filtered water from a natural source since Arizona almost a year earlier. There were a couple houses nearby, but nobody seemed to care if we camped on the beach.

As we were looking for a spot, a man yelled at us from the house. The man invited us up to the house. His name was Luis Alberto, and he said that it was OK to camp anywhere we liked on the beach, but instead he offered to let us sleep in his house. I asked him about his water and he said that he was on the same system, and it wasn't working either. Luis told me not to worry though; he had an old well and would bring us water from it. He was off with several large containers. Luis absolutely refused to let me help. He was insulted when I started walking to the well with him. He left Cindie and me enjoying the view of the ocean from his porch. He even had rocking chairs and beer for us. He returned with an enormous amount of water and climbed up on the roof. He filled a cistern and announced that our showers were ready.

Later that evening Luis said that we must have fresh coconut milk to sip on while we watched the sun set from his porch. Luis claimed to do exactly that every evening. He slung a machete over his back and quickly shimmied up a nearby palm tree. Near the top of the tree, he pulled out his machete and cut several coconuts free. They landed in the sand with a loud thud, and then he told us to be careful. Back on the ground Luis pulled his machete out again and hacked away at each coconut until it was a perfect drinking cup.

With our coconut milk in hand, we all watched the sun kiss the ocean and turn our tropical paradise into a show of colors. We both took showers and then setup our camping mattresses and sleeping bags in an empty room.

The next day of riding was hard because of the road and climbing temperatures. The road deteriorated to four-wheel drive only conditions. At a couple places, our track became so steep that I had to stand and grind my smallest gear (22 x 34) to the top. Then I laid my bike down and walked back to help Cindie push her rig. This extra effort in the tropical heat was draining. We rode all day to go a handful of kilometers.

Our destination was Playa Nosara where we could camp on the beach free. This was a small village with a great beach. We set our tent up at the beach and watched the birds celebrate the sunset. I like it best when we have absolutely nothing to do.

Playa Samara.

The ride to Playa Samara was much easier then the previous days grind thanks to an improved road and shade. As soon as we entered the camping area at Playa Samara, we were warned by the owner to watch our belongings. I noticed

Sunset at Playa Nosara.

287

Cindie on Playa Nosara, at sunrise.

that there were several tents left unattended and asked what those campers did with their valuables. I thought that he would tell me that there was a locker or security guard. He instead told me that the thieves wouldn't steal from Ticos (Costa Ricans). They prefer to steal from foreign tourists. This is a big problem in Costa Rican beach towns. This meant that one of us had to be with our tent at all times.

It was the weekend, so the campground was full of tents. We found a place in the shade and pitched our tent. Because of the warning from the campground owner, we took turns walking on the beach. This beach was popular with Ticos. Ticos love to surf; surfers with surfboards crowded the beach. We met dozens of Tico university students camping in the campground. It reminded me of American university students on spring break in Florida. We sat in the campground and discussed politics, music and the good surfing beaches in Costa Rica.

Our campsite at Playa Samara was empty during the week.

Road Warrior

We woke up before the sun rose and packed quietly so we wouldn't wake anyone else. We knew it was going to be another steamy day. As we climbed into the tropical coastal range we heard howler monkeys and green parrots in the trees making their regular morning noises. The parrots are the loudest; they fly in a group of ten or more, squawking in unison when they landed in a tree. The howler monkeys hollered to each other from an unseen place in the trees. The yell would start out low and increase in volume with each bellow.

On one of the downhills, we were cruising fast, and a large iguana jumped out in front of me. I didn't have time to stop or even veer away. I yelled, "Bump!" Because I knew Cindie, who was drafting off my rear wheel, would also hit it. I quickly braced myself for the impact. Iguanas down here are large things, between the size of a one-liter (0.26 gallon)

289

Iguana.

bottle and a two-liter (0.52 gallon) bottle. Fortunately, they are rather soft and squishy under the weight of our wheels. All I heard was thud thud – thud thud. I looked back to see Cindie wide-eyed but still on my wheel. I slowed down so she could come up next to me and talk about it. I didn't look back to check on the iguana because I was certain what his fate was: road kill.

Cindie asked me, "What was that?"

I told her that an iguana had darted in front of me in a successful attempt at suicide. We both felt bad for the big guy. We had become accustomed to them around our camp-sites, they were friendly, and didn't cause trouble.

We rode into Nicoya with sweat pouring off us at 10 a.m. Nicoya is a small town with an old colonial church on the square. We found a room off the square, carried our gear inside and promptly took a nap under the ceiling fan. The heat was getting to be more than an inconvenience – it was getting to be a health hazard. While planning the trip I had done my best to plan for the weather and made sure we were in Costa Rica during the dry season. What I hadn't taken into account was the tropical heat. If I ever return to Costa Rica on a bike it will be closer to the beginning of the dry season when the temperatures aren't so high.

We had one more riding day to get to the ferry. Not even the heat could spoil it. The road was flat and a strong wind pushed us along. We rode past rural Costa Rican life. Riding ferries with a bicycle is always an adventure for me, I never know if I will get seasick or not. The boat ride to Puntarenas was enjoyable because it was calm, and I didn't get sick.

Puntarenas, Costa Rica

As soon as we rolled off the ferry, I saw barbed wire across every rooftop and rusted steel bars covering all the windows. We rode past several beer and cigarette stalls lining the street. In front of these stalls, groups of young men stood around drinking local beer and smoking brands of cigarettes from every country a large ship can visit. They were bored and looking for something to do. We didn't want to be the entertainment for the day and kept moving.

Puntarenas, Costa Rica is an old port and a seedy transient town. This was evident with the abundance of fast living sailors who bring goods in their ships; these sailors mix with an equally rough bunch of truck drivers who mill around waiting for their trucks to be filled. This town had all the services to keep these workers happy. Every corner had a hard drinking bar that I dared not enter; however, I would have loved to have had a couple drinks with the boys to listen to marvelous stories about life on the open sea and in exotic distant ports.

All of these lonely men attracted professional ladies of the night who were hanging out at practically every street corner. They were friendly to say the least. Cindie must be able to communicate a lot of intimidation with one dirty look because they backed off quickly.

Finding a hotel room took forever. Many of the hotels catered to the late night crowd. Cindie found us a hotel that didn't charge by the hour, and we left this dangerous street scene behind. We only stayed one day.

We left Puntarenas before the sun came up and headed towards the most popular beach in Costa Rica, Playa Jaco. By 8 a.m., the temperature was over 85° Fahrenheit (29.5° Celsius) and the humidity was over 90%; it was unbearable. Our clothes were soaked from sweat, and we still hadn't climbed the big pass toward Playa Jaco.

We rode through Biological Reserve Carara and saw several sleepy alligators on the bank of a tropical river. They didn't care about anything. The real treat was the pair of scarlet macaws that flew past us. They were bright red and much larger (over two feet, 0.61 meters, high) than I expected. I thought birds like that only lived in pet stores. Oh, the things I get to see from the saddle.

Then we hit a steep hill a few kilometers outside of Playa Jaco. It wasn't that long or steep, but the unbearable high temperature and humidity was killing us. We were drinking tons of water and starting to run low. The signs of heat illness were appearing on both of us. Cindie was red in the face and had a headache. When we stopped, our body temperatures rose instead of dropping like we anticipated. The water in our water bottles was so hot we could have made tea. We had to stop several times to try to cool off. Even the shade was hot.

We spent over an hour climbing the small mountain. It was one of the hardest days on the trip. We talk about it often when the going gets tough. During a hard stretch, we say to each other, "This isn't so bad. Do you remember that miserable ride to Jaco back in March 2003?"

Costa Rica: Monkeys, Iguanas and Surfers

<u>Playa Jaco</u>

We were able to coast down the other side of the small mountain and cool off. At least we could think more clearly. One of the first things we saw, as we rode into town, was a Pizza Hut with a sign in English claiming to have air conditioning. We both pulled in without saying a word to each other. At this point, we had been on the road long enough that some things didn't need to be said.

Unfortunately, heading south in the spring would surely get hotter. I was increasingly feeling like I had made a big mistake in our planning.

Playa Jaco, Costa Rica's most popular beach is the closest beach to San Jose, a city of three million and Costa Rica's capital. Jaco was the most expensive and tacky place that we went in Costa Rica.

We found the huge centrally located campground and paid more than we had for most hotel rooms to the north. We were told not to leave any valuables in our tent because they would be stolen. At least this campground had a lock up. Whenever the two of us would leave, we would put the computer, camera, shortwave radio and all the rest of our important belongings in a dry bag and lock it up. Other less expensive things like our stove and sleeping bags were left in the tent and we locked our bikes to a tree. We stayed for several days, enjoyed the beach and had no problems with theft.

We woke up before the sun and started another rolling sunrise. As we rode out of Jaco, the only people awake were at the all-night disco. They hadn't gone to bed yet. We stopped at a red light directly in front of the party crowd. All eyes in the disco were on us, and we waved back. Obviously, we have different ambitions compared to most other tourists.

We were going to a predetermined place called Rancho Mastatal to meet Cindie's twin sister Cherie and her nine-year-old son James.

The road rambled south past numerous empty beaches and hidden villages. Then we turned inland on a dusty dirt road. We had trouble finding the correct road and actually rode in a complete circle. This wasted the remainder of the morning's cooler hours. The steep dirt sections caused us to overheat, and we had to stop. We found the right road and put in only a few miserable kilometers before my rear tire went flat. That was the last straw. I worked at changing the tube, but the heat was slowing me down, and I couldn't think. This was a low point for the both of us.

In the midst of hitting bottom, a pickup truck stopped, and the driver asked if we needed help. This was a case of meeting the right person at the right time. He gave us water and openly told us that we looked bad. He asked us if we wanted a ride. Our reply was a defeated yes. We loaded our bikes and gear into the bed of his pickup truck and were zooming up into the mountains.

Rancho Mastatal

The driver of the truck kindly dropped us off on the doorstep of Rancho Mastatal. The ranch is a hidden place and would have been difficult to find on our bicycles. Even though we had gained altitude, we were still in the rainforest. It's a quiet eco-tourist retreat. While we were there, it was busy with a group from the USA who came on a two-week workshop. They were learning about local building techniques.

Cindie best describes the arrival of her family to the ranch from her daily journal.

Cherie and James were supposed to arrive at 1:00 a.m. I woke up at 12:30 a.m. and heard a car drive up the road, and I knew they were here. I was still half-asleep when I started up the trail towards the front gate and the truck; I rubbed my left eye and out popped my contact. Now I was running down the path half-blind and half-asleep. As I stumbled down the path, I prayed there were no snakes in my way.

Cherie and James arrived in a huge commotion with slamming doors and loud voices. I had to quiet everyone down before we went back to the campsite because other people were sleeping in tents around us. We were excited to see each other; we hadn't seen each other in a year.

We woke up late and had breakfast at the ranch: fresh yogurt, papaya, watermelon and homemade bread. We walked down to the swimming hole and saw a group of three Grisons, an animal that is shaped like a weasel and has the markings of a skunk; it was an animal rarely seen by tourists. While swimming, Cherie and James saw a peccary (pig-like), a cane toad and a common anole. In the evening, Cherie and I went birding; we saw a White-fronted Parrot and Chestnut-mandible Toucan. We decided birding was something we would like to do more often together.

The next day Cindie, Cherie and I hired a local guide to take us on a private hike and point out the unique wildlife in the rainforest. Our guide's name was Chepo, and he was a short, muscular, hard working man. Chepo had lived in these mountains all of his life and knew the local animal and plant life well.

During our hike, Chepo reached into a bush and pulled out a black and green poison dart frog. Chepo seemed to know how to handle the frog and held it in his hand for us to get a closer look. I think that the frog is only poisonous when eaten. We also saw the beautiful blue Morph butterfly and a wide variety of tropical plants. After the hike James and Anaya, Chepo's daughter, played for hours. I liked how well the kids played together even when they didn't know a word of each other's language.

Cindie, Cherie and James went on a horseback ride at 8:00 a.m. This was James' first time. The horses were working horses used for rounding up cattle, not the usual trail horses that are found at stables in the USA. Tim (ranch owner) gave James a great demonstration on how to ride a horse. As soon as he related steering a horse to operating a joystick (hand held video game controller), James understood the concept immediately. James was controlling his horse within twenty minutes.

One evening Chepo led a group of other guests on a night hike through the rainforest. They came back excited because they had seen a fer-de-lance snake. The fer-de-lance snake is the most poisonous snake in Central America; its bite is fatal to humans. Chepo killed it because it was too close to people's homes in the area.

Cindie, Cherie, James and Chepo.

Chepo with a black poison dart frog.

Blue morph butterfly.

Back to Jaco

Because Cherie and James didn't have bikes, we hired a truck and piled our bikes in the back to make the trip to Jaco. We all enjoyed the beach and local shopping. We also went to Costa Rica's most famous national park, Manual Antonio.

We set out for Manual Antonio at 6:30 a.m.; James was still asleep but managed to get on the bus where he slept all the way to the national park. We were in luck, the park was brimming with wildlife: I think everything was out because it had been raining for the past few days and finally the sun was out. We saw the Jesus Christ Basilisk (a lizard that runs so fast he can run across the water), three-toed sloth (they are shy and move slow), iguana (they are as big as a small poodle), white throated capuchin monkey (they were aggressive because people feed them), tropical crab (they were everywhere), long-nosed bat and hermit crab. We brought

Beach at San Manual Antonio Park.

298

White faced capuchin monkey .

Three toed sloth.

our swimsuits and spent the hot part of the day swimming.

From Jaco we took a bus and taxi truck far up into the mountains to the village of Santa Elena. When the truck stopped at a hostel in Santa Elena, we opened the doors, and we were relieved to feel a burst of cool air. It felt like air conditioning, but the cool air was really the effect of the altitude. My headache I had developed during the weeks in hot weather faded away.

We spent a busy week enjoying the cool temperatures and seeing the many sights. This area is home to the Monteverde and Santa Elena Cloud Forest National Parks.

Monteverde is a Quaker community that was founded in 1951. The Quakers began dairy farming and buying property in the area. The Monteverde Cloud Forest was born, and they continue today to purchase land to enlarge the reserve. The nearby Santa Elena Cloud forest reserve is younger and closer to Volcano Arenal. One of the hikes goes to a tower where you can see and hear the volcano. On cloudy days, the rumbling of the volcano can be heard while hiking the many trails through the cloud forest.

Cherie and James did the Sky Trek Canopy tour while in Santa Elena. Sky Trek or zip line is a series of towers connected by a heavy cable. Riders zip along on a pulley system from one tower to the next. It cost $40 for an adult and $32 for a child. We passed because it was out of our budget. They came back still pumped with adrenaline. James (eight) was the youngest that they would take on the canopy tour. He said, "It made my eyes water like crazy." Cherie had a great time as well.

That evening we went to the Ranario, also known as the frog pond. We saw all kinds of frogs, including the blue jeans frog (they are red with blue legs), green jeans (red with green legs), the green and black poison dart frog and numerous other frogs. My favorite was the red-eyed leaf frogs. They are extremely active at night, and the acrobatics they perform while moving around in their terrarium are a delight to watch.

Decision Not to Ride to Panama City

After Cherie and James left, we had planned to spend the remaining three weeks riding to Panama City, Panama because of the departure date of our air flight we had purchased several weeks before. We planned to fly from Panama City to the USA to visit our families. Leaving Santa Elena was difficult. We had much to see and do, and the weather was invitingly cool. We could take hikes every day and not overheat in the sun.

Riding south through the remainder of Costa Rica and Panama would mean enduring increasingly hot and humid weather. From our experiences in the heat during the last month, we had grown to fear hot humid riding and not being able to sleep at night. Besides, three weeks wasn't much

Red eyed tree frog.

Red eyed tree frog on the glass of the terrarium.

time for us to cover this distance. We like to enjoy ourselves and that is difficult if we feel rushed. The only way to ride that far and fast would be to ride on the main highway and share our days with noise and traffic. Many of the interesting sights are far off the main road and would have to be passed.

There was another option. We could stay in the paradise of Santa Elena and take the bus to Panama City. A convenient first class bus company had frequent direct bus connections to Panama City. The big dilemma was that we originally had planned to ride the entire way. It seemed like we would be cheating if we finished on the bus.

We thought long and hard about this. We asked ourselves, "Is it important to ride the whole way? Whom is this trip for and whom are we trying to impress?" The answer was obvious. This trip was for our enjoyment and we weren't trying to impress anyone. We chose to stay and enjoy paradise for another three weeks instead of grinding through the inferno to impress others.

We loved staying in Santa Elena. We had time to visit and revisit the major sights in the area and to see some of the off-the-beaten-track activities. We were tired of riding the bikes, so we went on daily hikes for our exercise. We actively sought and found the shy colorful birds such as Toucans and Quetzals. The time we spent in Santa Elena was one of the most peaceful and relaxing periods during our journey. Besides having fun I spent hours writing and working on our Web site, www.downtheroad.org. This book wouldn't have been possible without that extended time to write.

We could have stayed longer, but we reluctantly packed and caught a bus for the long ride to Panama City, Panama. During our transfer of buses in San Jose, Costa Rica, a funny thing happened. When the passengers were unloading their luggage from the bus, our bikes and boxes were last. As I went to grab our belongings the attendant told me that I would have to pay him first. I told him that none of the other passengers was required to pay, and I am no different. I think he was surprised that I was able to challenge him in Spanish. He stalled and asked for a smaller amount hoping things would turn his way. To end the matter I offered to visit the bus company's office in the bus terminal, pay his boss and ask for a receipt. He suddenly changed his mind about the payment and quickly unloaded our belongings and sent us on our way.

Tropical size cockroach.

Zebra butterfly.

14 Panama: Not without My Bike

(April 12 – 17, 2003)

We stayed a week in the cosmopolitan Panama City, Panama and had many places to visit including the Panama Canal and the old historic section of the city.

US Dollar

The strange thing about the country of Panama is that they abandoned their own currency and adopted the US dollar as their official currency. This meant that all the prices are in dollars and easier for us. It was strange to see our money in a foreign country. This in no way bothers me – I thought it was strange. If I were Panamanian, I would feel that giving up my national currency was giving up part of my country's sovereignty. When I asked locals about this, they had mixed reactions. One said, that now their currency does not devalue as quickly while another said he missed the old currency and didn't like being tied so close to the USA. El Salvador and Ecuador are two other countries that have adopted the US dollar as their official currency.

The main attraction in Panama City was the internationally famous Panama Canal. We took a taxi out to the canal and stayed the entire day watching huge ships, with only inches to spare, pass through the locks like toys in a bathtub. In the elaborate visitors' center we learned the Panamanian perspective of the canal's history. Panama had to first break away from Colombia, and then the French tried to build the canal. Malaria and yellow fever conquered the French attempt and left behind a daunting cemetery of twenty thousand filled with victims of these tropical diseases.

Panama City

Boats passing through the Panama Canal.

Leaving Panama With Our Bikes

Flying in a jet requires partially disassembling each bike and packing it in a bike box. I have done this a few times in foreign countries and usually experienced a time-consuming hassle. Panama City must see regular air bound cyclists because it took only a visit to one of the many modern bike shops to arrange to have the work done. It was cheap, fast and the mechanic did a great job.

The day we went to the airport was one of the craziest days on the trip. It started out simple enough with us loading our boxed bikes into a taxi and going to the airport three hours ahead of time. In the airport, we waited in a long line while a dog sniffed our luggage and a human airport screener opened everything while looking for drugs and weapons. The Panama City Airport is working hard to lose its reputation as a drug exporter. After being deemed fit to fly, we walked up to the check-in counter. There they told us that our bikes couldn't fly with us.

This was highly irregular. We have flown many times in the past on that same airline with boxed bikes, sometimes we had to pay extra, but we were always able to bring our bikes. We were told that we would have to ship the bikes through the air cargo terminal. I politely asked to see a manager. After our extended plea she still told us "No." She wouldn't even accept my monetary motivation.

We had to get our bikes to the cargo airport and back before our flight took off. Cindie paid our exit tax while I hailed another cab. We were off on the twenty-minute drive to the air cargo terminal. We were stopped at the front gate to the terminal. The checkpoint guard told us that if we didn't work in the terminal, we couldn't pass. I told him the entire story about our bikes not being allowed to fly with us and how the airline manager told us to take the bikes to the air cargo terminal. He was uninterested in my story until I produced US$5, then he completely changed his tune and let us pass. When I returned to the cab Cindie asked me how I talked them into letting us through. I told her that I had used a "Lincoln Pass." We pulled up to the terminal office. All these delays ate up more time.

I knew that it was a waste of time to speak to the employees and went straight to the manager. I, again, told the entire story about how we weren't allowed to fly with our bikes. He told me that the terminal was for commercial freight that was first processed through an export broker and this takes several days. Cindie became extremely upset and unruly. We had only forty-five minutes to catch our flight, and her coming unglued wasn't helping. I had to ask her to wait outside with the bikes.

I asked the manager if I could speak with someone higher up the corporate ladder. He dialed the phone and spoke in English while asking for a person by name. He never had told me that he spoke English. Eventually, I was handed the phone and found myself talking with a corporate manager in the USA. I explained our situation and time frame. He told me the exact words that I wanted to hear: "I will take care of it."

By now, we had thirty minutes to catch our plane. We threw our bikes back in the waiting cab and offered to double the fare if he could get us back to the airport on time. The driver flew into the passenger terminal, screeched to a halt and helped me carry the bikes back to the check-in desk. The same manager who told us to go to the air cargo terminal met us and was now apologetic. I could tell that she had received a phone call from upper management in the USA. This time our bikes were easily checked in, and she personally escorted us through immigration and screening. As we were walking up to the gate, she asked me if we had US$100 cash per bike to pay for transport. I stalled and explained that we didn't have any cash on us but had a credit card. I knew that it would be severely bad for her career if we didn't make our flight and that there was no time to process a credit card. She told me to forget it, and we boarded the plane. It seemed as if the plane was taxiing before we even found our seat. We sat down, buckled up and were in the air.

Once settled in our seats, we could catch our breath. We now had time to discuss what had happened to us on our trip so far. It had been a little over a year since we had begun our journey and, in that short time, our lifestyle and way of thinking had been turned upside down. I thought back to the beginning and how green and naive we were. This first leg of our journey had been everything we had expected, and it had revealed an unexpected deeper meaning about the world. We had thought our way of life was the only way to live. Now we had seen that there were many different ways that people conducted their lives.

We Can Do This

First, we had learned that we could live on bicycles and fulfill our dreams of traveling the globe. We had learned how to efficiently pack our bikes, pass through borders with bribes, hide on the side of the road in a tent at night, avoid pickpockets and bandits, and survive in aggressive, polluted Latin American city traffic. We had gained important experience in international travel and were able to operate within unfamiliar customs and cultures.

Our new knowledge and skills will be put to use in the coming years as we continue riding our bicycles through many different parts of the world.

Living on a bike taught us to live on a basic level. Most luxuries such as refrigerators, televisions, hair gel and a large wardrobe of clothing we have learned to do without. We discovered how life can be more with less.

Cindie and I learned how to work together to overcome whatever we encountered, including illness, violent storms and personal differences. Every obstacle can be overcome when we remain calm, think before we act and work as a team. Our practice in confronting the unknown was making it easier. This self-confidence will carry us through the darkest of times. Knowing that we can deal with whatever comes our way is extremely empowering.

We can do this!

I also learned about myself in several ways. Physically I discovered how far I could push myself and how much I could suffer through. I discovered how much dirty laundry and how many infrequent and cold showers I can tolerate. I don't have to live the pampered life that I once had expected in the USA. I can survive and be content on far less. The more challenges I am forced to face, the stronger I become. It's not bad to sweat on a regular basis.

The long silent hours and months on the bikes had given us the opportunity to think. We'd had time, like it or not, to look deep within ourselves and criticize our flaws. I have found that the more I understand other people, the more I understand myself. This is helping me define myself and explain how I fit in the world. A career no longer defines me; I am defined instead by the experiences and knowledge I gain. Wealth is no longer measured by numbers in a bank account but instead by memories captured in my photo album and writings. These things are far more valuable than money.

We discovered that our seven-year travel plan is financially realistic. The entire first year cost ten thousand dollars US, which is much less than we expected. This means we have time and money to travel more than the original seven years. The world is a big place, and we are looking forward to seeing as much of it as we can with the money we have left. We both agree that we want to continue until our bodies give out. We are addicted.

Panama: Not without My Bike

We discovered that the world outside the borders of our own country wasn't what we had been led to believe. People in our country told us that we wouldn't be safe south of the border and that poor people would only want to steal from us. We found the people of that part of the world generally to be wonderful but in any society there are always a sprinkling of nasty individuals. I believe that people in the USA suffer from a great unfounded fear of the outside world. We believed these fears ourselves until we gained firsthand experience outside the country. It was crushing and embarrassing to learn that our concept of the world was fictitious. We never realized how many misconceptions and false stereotypes we had believed while living in the USA. We are now working hard at finding the truth, but it's not always what we want to hear.

Life on the road was far from the horror that we had expected, but not as perfect as some idealistic travelers would lead you to believe. We found good and bad aspects in every country we visited and the various cultures we encountered. We didn't find the perfect way of life at home or on the road.

We learned the true nature of "poverty" and how the meaning of "happiness" is as individual as the people we met, and yet all humans have the same basic needs and wants. We learned what it really meant to be from the developed world. The benefit from my nationality isn't the perceived wealth but instead the opportunities that I have contrasted to those living in the underdeveloped world.

I thought of the privileged lifestyle that we had before we left with guilt. Most people in the world are happier with far fewer material possessions. With only what we could carry on our bikes to call ours we focused in on the things that really matter in life. This is another unexpected gift from the road.

Many things that I once thought to be important are now irrelevant because I see them through new eyes after this initial journey. I don't need to impress anyone with how many things I own, how fast I can ride a bike or how many miles I covered on this trip. Those things are silly compared to the experience of learning about people and their lives that are so different from my own.

Yes, this first leg of our trip literally changed my life. The only thing that I am sure of now is that I will continue to change and grow as I travel through more countries with different cultures on this road that has no end.

Kuna women in old Panama city.

Our Second Book

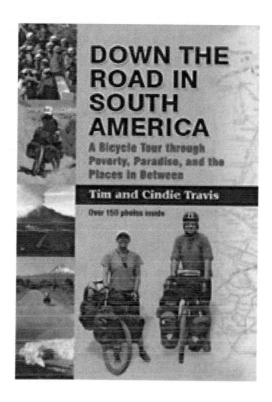

"Down The Road in South America: A Bicycle Tour Through Poverty , Paradise, and the Places in Between."

ISBN: 978-9754427-3-9

284 pages

over 180 black and white photos

includes an equipment packing list

Available in Paperback and eBook at our web site:

www.downtheroad.org

Lightning Source UK Ltd.
Milton Keynes UK
22 September 2010

160196UK00001B/133/P